Welcome To

# MY ENGLISH PROF.

## A Comprehensive ESL Guide

Zeenam Irshad

**BLUEROSE PUBLISHERS**
India | U.K.

Copyright © Zeenam Irshad 2025

All rights reserved by author. No part of this publication may be reproduced, stored in a retrieval system or transmitted in any form or by any means, electronic, mechanical, photocopying, recording or otherwise, without the prior permission of the author. Although every precaution has been taken to verify the accuracy of the information contained herein, the publisher assumes no responsibility for any errors or omissions. No liability is assumed for damages that may result from the use of information contained within.

BlueRose Publishers takes no responsibility for any damages, losses, or liabilities that may arise from the use or misuse of the information, products, or services provided in this publication.

For permissions requests or inquiries regarding this publication,
please contact:

BLUEROSE PUBLISHERS
www.BlueRoseONE.com
info@bluerosepublishers.com
+91 8882 898 898
+4407342408967

ISBN: 978-93-7018-005-5

First Edition: May 2025

# DEDICATED

## " To my Dad,

Whose unwavering support and encouragement guided me to study Post Graduation Diploma in English Language Teaching. Your desire to make learning English easier for others has been my ultimate inspiration. Thank you for your belief in me and in this mission."

Md. Zabiulla
RTD,Teacher
Malladihalli

# Foreword

A few Fore words…

When I heard a sweet smooth sophisticated voice of Zeenam requesting me to write a few lines as a foreword for her book on English grammar, I didn't have any tall presumption about the book my past student might have written. I could never fore see that, this tiny girl then, who was studying the Commerce subjects in Kannada medium (except Accountancy, all other subjects were taught in Kannada medium in our PU college, Malladihalli), could conquer a foreign language like English, to write a book on its grammar. Infact, when she handed the neatly printed pages spirally bound, I took it into my hands with a mocking smile on my lips.

Later, when opened the pages and started to tread lazily through the pages, I stood stunned and realized that our tiny student has grown enormously. I really felt surprised and gasping to comprehend how our Zeenam, brought up in a remote backward rural area, could achieve such in-depth fluency in a foreign language like English. Whatever might be the reasons for my earlier casual attitudes towards her book, the pages in my hands made me to feel proud, and produced a happy smile on my face.

***

This book wrote by Zeenam is of germinal nature. Like the minute seed of the great Banyan tree of English language, it contains all the aspects of the language in germinal form, that can sprout to flourish and give us a confident fluency in the use of English language. The book deals all the grammatic aspects of English language, that can surely help any reader to learn the correct use of English language.

The book starts with a chapter on Alphabet. Dealing with their classification the discussion treads further to suggest the phonetic aspects of the language. I doesn't end there! I later part of the book, the chapter, `Pronunciation Guide', more aspects of the phonetics of the speech are given. A short list of words, classified grammatically, will definitely help the readers to acquire the basic vocabulary as well as a confident and proper speaking ability of the English.

I am immensely impressed about the practical usefulness of this book. It is very useful for both the learners and teachers of the English at the elementary schools.

I earnestly feel proud of Zeenam and express my hearty congratulations for her successful endeavor in producing this book.

**Prof. Raghavendra Patil**

http://raghavendrapatil.in/

# PREFACE

Welcome to MY ENGLISH PROF., a comprehensive guide designed to help learners of all ages master the essentials of English grammar and improve their language skills. Whether you're just beginning your English-learning journey or looking to refine your understanding.

In this book, you'll find step-by-step lessons covering various aspects of English grammar, from the basics of sentence structure to more advanced concepts. I have also included tips, and real-world examples to help you apply what you learn in everyday communication.

I hope this book serves as both a helpful tool and an inspiring companion in your journey to becoming more confident and proficient in English. It is my belief that learning a language opens doors to new opportunities, and I am excited to be part of your learning experience.

**Remember, learning grammar is not just about following rules—it's about gaining the tools to express yourself effectively and confidently in any situation.**

Thank you for choosing MY ENGLISH PROF. Let's embark on this grammatical journey together!

## ACKNOWLEDGEMENTS

I am profoundly honored to extend my heartfelt gratitude to **Raghavendra Patil Sir**, a brilliant writer whose eloquent words continue to inspire and enrich the literary world. Your gracious contribution in crafting the foreword for My English Prof. is a testament to your generosity and deep understanding of the written word. Your insightful reflections have not only elevated this book but also reignited my passion for writing. Your support and encouragement bring immense value to this work, and I will remain forever grateful for your kindness and wisdom.

**To explore his work and contributions, please visit...**   http://raghavendrapatil.in/

To my **Husband**, thank you for being my biggest cheerleader and for always believing in me. Your unwavering support and encouragement have made this book possible.

To my **Mother**, your boundless love, and Support have been the cornerstone of my journey. Both of you have been my greatest sources of strength and inspiration, and I am forever grateful for your belief in me.

*I would also like to thank my mentors and to all of you who have made this journey possible, thank you.,*

ZEENAM

# CONTENTS

## 01 All About Alphabet — 10
- 44 Speech Sounds — 12
- Consonant Blends, — 20
- Digraphs — 22
- Spelling Rules — 23

## 02 The Word — 34
- Types of Words
- Capitalization Rules — 35
- Prefixes and Suffixes — 36
- Syllables & Syllable Division Rules — 40
- The Articles "A, An & The — 43

## 03 The Sentence — 45
- Types of Sentences
- Punctuation in Sentences — 49

## 04 Parts of Speech — 51
- Noun and Types of Noun — 53
- Pronoun and Types — 61
- Adjective and Types — 68
- Degrees of comparison — 78
- Verb and Types — 81
- Modal and helping verbs — 84
- Adverb and Types — 106
- Preposition — 112
- Conjuction — 119
- Interjection — 123

## 05 Figures of Speech — 126
- Simile — 127
- Metaphor — 128
- Hyperbole — 130
- alliteration — 131

## 06

**The Tense** — 134
Direct and indirect speech — 138
Active Voice and Passive Voice — 141
Question forms — 143
Punctuation — 146

**Synonyms and Antonyms** — 147
**Idioms and Phrases** — 157

## 07

**Composition** — 162
Letter Writing — 163
Essay — 168
Precis — 177
Paraphrase — 190

## 08

**Pronunciation Guide** — 188
Manner of Articulation
IPA Pronunciation Chart

**Basic Vocabulary** — 194
**Adjectives and Opposites** — 199
**Verbs and their tense forms** — 212

## Conclusion — 219

# Skills of Learning

Learning a new language is an exciting journey, and mastering English as a second language (ESL) requires a combination of skills that work together to help you succeed. In this book, we will explore key skills that are essential for effective language learning. These include listening, speaking, reading, and writing, each of which plays a vital role in your understanding and communication. Along with these core skills, we will also cover strategies for improving vocabulary, grammar, and pronunciation, helping you to become a confident English speaker. Whether you are a beginner or looking to refine your skills, these learning techniques will guide you on your path to fluency.

## Listening

The ability to understand spoken language is essential for communication. This skill involves not only hearing the words but also comprehending their meanings, nuances, and context. Listening skills help learners grasp pronunciation, intonation, and rhythm, which are vital for understanding and being understood in conversations.

## Speaking

Speaking is the ability to express oneself orally in the target language. This skill involves using correct pronunciation, grammar, vocabulary, and appropriate expressions to convey ideas effectively. Practice in speaking helps learners become more fluent and confident in real-life communication situations.

## Reading

Reading involves understanding written text in the target language. It requires recognizing and interpreting words, phrases, sentences, and longer passages. Reading skills help learners expand their vocabulary, improve comprehension, and gain insights into grammar and sentence structure.

## Writing

Writing is the ability to produce written text in the target language. This skill encompasses spelling, grammar, punctuation, vocabulary choice, and coherence. Writing practice helps learners reinforce their understanding of language rules, express their thoughts clearly and accurately, and develop their own style of writing.

# All About ALPHABET

**Aa** is for apple — make a sound "aeh"

**Bb** is for banana — make a sound "buh"

**Cc** is for cat — make a sound "kuh"

**Dd** is for dog — make a sound "duh"

**Ee** is for egg — make a sound "eh"

**Ff** is for fish — make a sound "fff"

**Gg** is for gate — make a sound "guh"

**Hh** is for hat — make a sound "huh"

**Ii** is for igloo — make a sound "ihh"

**Jj** is for jelly — make a sound "juh"

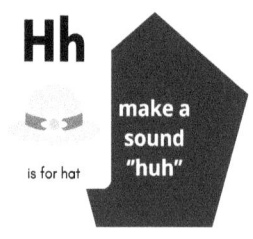
**Kk** is for kite — make a sound "kuh"

**Ll** is for lemon — make a sound "lll"

## Mm

is for monkey
make a sound "mmm"

## Nn

is for net
make a sound "nn"

## Oo

is for orange
make a sound "o"

## Pp

is for pear
make a sound "puh"

## Qq

is for queen
make a sound "qwah"

## Rr

is for rabbit
make a sound "rr"

## Ss

is for strawberry
make a sound 'sss'

## Tt

is for tiger
make a sound "tt"

## Uu

is for umbrella
make a sound "uh"

## Vv

is for van
make a sound "vuh"

## Ww

is for whale
make a sound "wuh"

## Xx

is for x-ray
make a sound "kks"

## Yy

is for yoyo
make a sound "yuh"

## Zz

is for zebra
make a sound 'zz'

VOWELS
a e i o u * y

CONSONANTS
b c d f g h j k l m n p q r s t v w x z

The 44 speech sounds in English as defined by the International Phonetic Alphabet (IPA). These are:

## Consonant Sounds

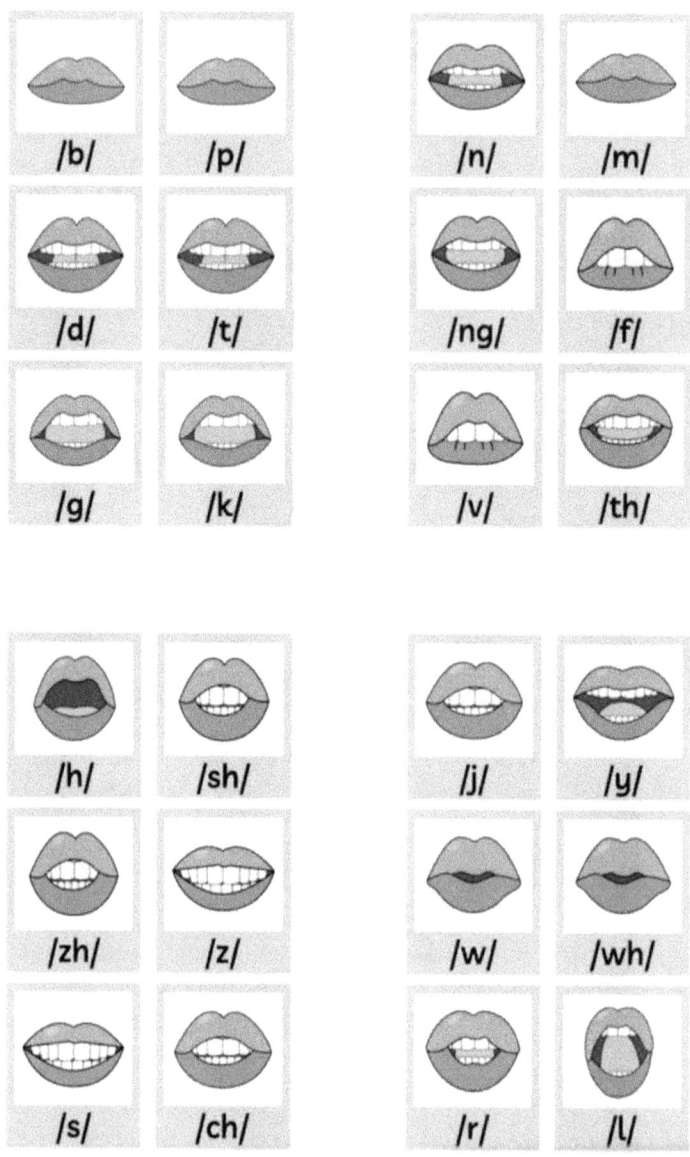

"Refer to the Pronunciation Guide for articulation guidelines of each sound."

# Consonant Sounds: 24

**p** — Pen, past, post, support

**b** — Book, nib, grabbed

**t** — Tea, winter, asked,

**j** — Jug, jump, jet

**d** — Dog, did, begged

**k/c** — Kite, corn, chaos,

**g** — Gun, girl, g as j (gem, gym,)

**T as ch** — Chin, nature, nurture

**Ph as f** — Phone, photo, film, fish

**v** — Victory, veil, visit

**th** — Think, thin, path

**th** — Those, these, this

**S and c** — Nose, lace, space

**Z and s** — Zebra, zoo, those, dogs

**Sh and t** — Shoot, shut, nation, mention

**sz** — Vision, pleasure,

**h** — Hot, hat, hit

**m** — Man, thumb, lamb

**n** — Net, not, pneumonia

**n (ng)** — Finger, singer, longer

**l** — Lap, nil, pulled

**r** — Rat, river, ring

**y (j)** — Yet, yellow

**w** — Water, wait, twist

# Vowel Sounds

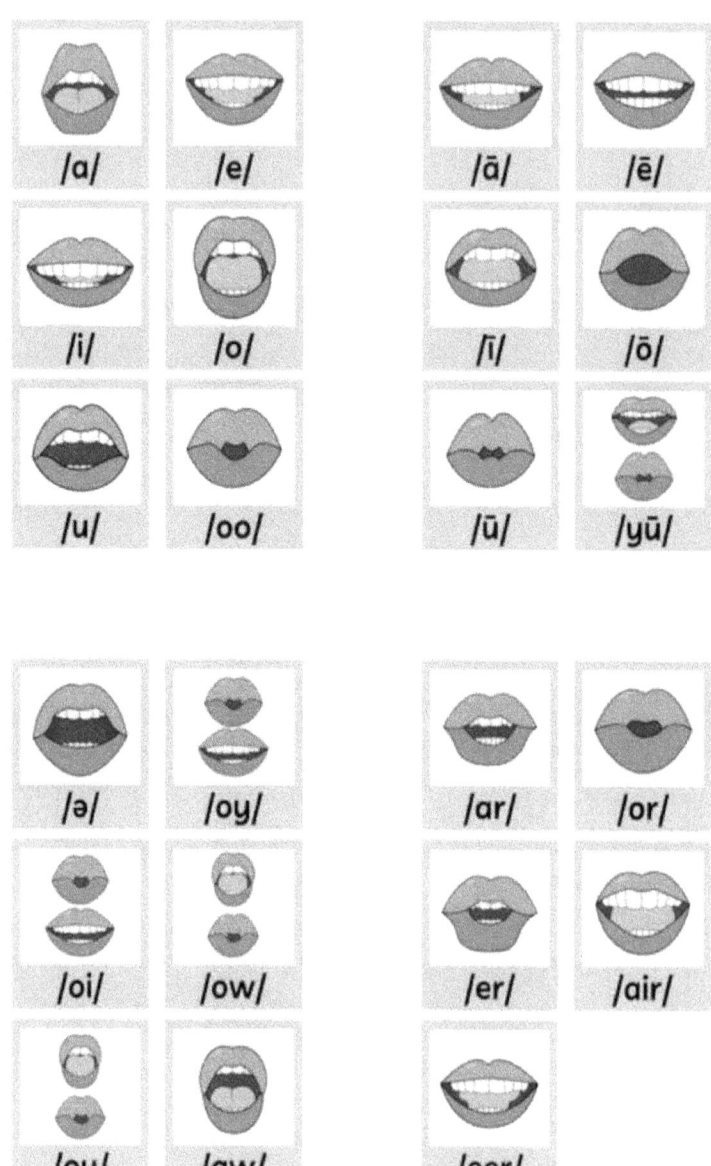

"Refer to the Pronunciation Guide for articulation guidelines of each sound."

# Vowel Sounds (20)

## Short Vowel Sounds

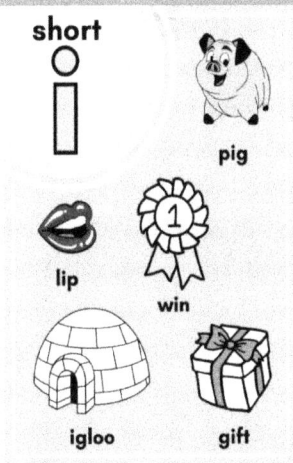
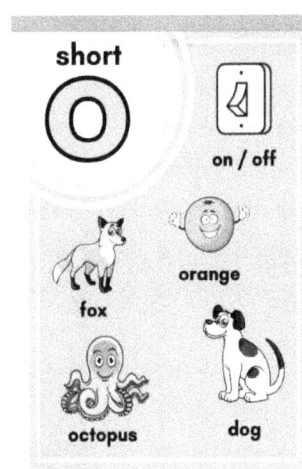

- Cake
- Mate
- Game
- Rain
- Train
- Sail
- Play
- Snake
- Gray
- Stay
- Break
- Steak
- Age
- Brave
- Name
- Plate
- Chain
- Wait
- Day
- Today
- Late
- State
- Bay
- Frame
- Gate
- Wave
- Pave
- Trail
- Pray
- Plane

- See
- Tree
- Free
- Bee
- Sea
- Leaf
- Key
- Three
- Cheese
- Green
- Breeze
- Evening
- Believe
- Achleve
- Peace
- Read
- Scream
- Stream
- Beach
- Heat
- Feet
- Meat
- Team
- Wheel
- Seal
- Deal
- Meal
- Dream
- Sneeze
- Please

- Kite
- Pie
- Bike
- Light
- Night
- Ice
- Time
- High
- Lie
- Cry
- Try
- Fight
- Right
- Bright
- Sky
- Five
- Drive
- Smile
- Line
- Side
- Shine
- Find
- Slide
- Wide
- Flight
- Dry
- Tie
- Style
- Fire
- Height

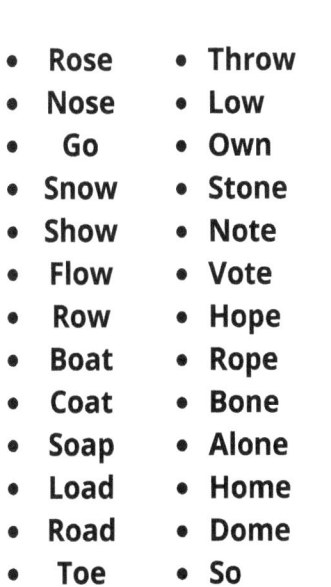

- Rose
- Nose
- Go
- Snow
- Show
- Flow
- Row
- Boat
- Coat
- Soap
- Load
- Road
- Toe
- Know
- Grow
- Throw
- Low
- Own
- Stone
- Note
- Vote
- Hope
- Rope
- Bone
- Alone
- Home
- Dome
- So
- Glow
- Froze

- Cube
- Tune
- Mule
- Fuse
- Flute
- Rule
- June
- Use
- Cute
- Huge
- True
- Blue
- Due
- Glue
- Sue

- Few
- View
- News
- Rescue
- Venue
- Queue
- Value
- Tissue
- Issue
- Argue
- Avenue
- Barbecue
- Pursue
- Continue
- Statue

# 4 SOUNDS OF Y

yolk — y as consonant — at beginning of a word

cherry — y as long e — at end in 2 syllable word

gym — y as short i — in middle of a word

cry — y as long i — at end in 1 syllable word

# DIPHTHONGS

A diphthong is two vowels that work together to make a new vowel sound.

| OI | | OY | |
|---|---|---|---|
| coins | point | joy | destroy |
| **OU** | | **OW** | |
| sound | house | town | howl |
| **AU** | | **AW** | |
| pause | sauce | paw | saw |
| **OO** | | **U** | |
| books | cookie | push | bush |

## Phonics Fun

In a land where letters play,
Each sound has a role today.
Come along and sing with me,
Let's explore our ABCs!

**Ch** is for cheese and chair,
**Sh** is for shoes that we wear.
**Th** can be soft as in then,
Or hard like this with a grin.

**Ai** says a in a rainy day,
**Ea** in a leaf where the children play.
**Oa** in a boat that sails so far,
**Ou** in clouds and shouting stars.

**Bl** is for blue and black,
**Tr** is for train on the track.
**Fl** is for flower blooming bright,
**St** is for star that lights the night.

**Ar** in a car and star so high,
**Or** in a cornfield under the sky.
**Er** in her and term we learn,
**Ir** in bird as it takes a turn.

Blend the sounds and blend the fun,
With each letter, there's a new one.
Read the words and spell them right,
Phonics makes our reading bright!

# Consonant Blends

## Beginning Blends

| bl | cl | fl | gl |
|---|---|---|---|
| black | clap | flower | glue |
| pl | sl | br | cr |
| plant | slide | brush | crown |
| dr | fr | gr | pr |
| drum | frog | grapes | prince |
| tr | sc | sm | sn |
| tree | scooter | smile | snail |
| sp | st | sw | tw |
| spoon | star | swan | twig |

## Ending Blends

| | | |
|---|---|---|
| **ct**  act | **ft**  gift | **ld**  gold |
| **lf**  wolf | **lk**  milk | **lp**  help |
| **lt**  salt | **mp**  lamp | **nd**  band |
| **nk** 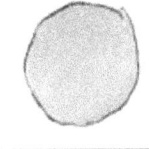 pink | **nt** 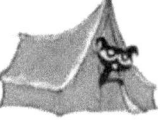 tent | **pt**  slept |
| **sk**  desk | **rp**  harp | **st**  nest |
| **rd**  bird | **rk**  fork | **lb**  bulb |
| **rm**  arm | **rn**  yarn | **rt** 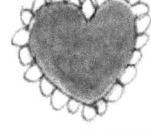 heart |

# DIGRAPHS

A pair of letters that make one sound.

**SH**: ship, push, sharp, sheep, shell, wish, crash

**PH**: phone, graph, photo, dolphin, trophy, sphere, nephew

**WH**: white, whale, when, where, why, which, wheel

**CH**: chip, cheap, catch, itch, fetch, choke, cheat

**TH**: thing, bath, pith, thank, truth

## Trigraphs

| DGE | IGH | TCH |
|---|---|---|
| Bridge | Sigh | Catch |
| badge | Night | Batch |
| Fridge | Flight | Hatch |
| Edge | Thigh | Fetch |
| Hedge | High | Kitchen |
| Judge | Tight | Pitch |
| Lodge | Bright | Ditch |
| Hedge | Right | Witch |
| Ridge | Might | Sketch |
| Fudge | Sunlight | Match |

## Quadgraphs

| AUGH | OUGH | EIGH |
|---|---|---|
| Laugh | Dough | Eight |
| Draught | Though | Weigh |
| Distraught | Bought | Sleigh |
| Slaughter | Thought | Height |
| Aught | Fought | Inveigh |
| Caught | Through | Weight |
| Taught | Borough | Outweigh |
| Naughty | Thorough | Eighteen |
| Fraught | Tough | Freight |
| Daughter | Enough | Neigh |

# Spelling Rules

## I Before E Except After C

Rule : "i" usually comes before "e" except after "c" or when sounding like "a."
Examples: believe, receive, friend, ceiling, but: weigh, eight

## Drop the Final E Before Adding a Suffix

Rule : When adding a suffix that begins with a vowel to a word ending in "e," drop the final "e.
Examples:
- make → making
- hope → hoping

## Double the Final Consonant Before Adding a Suffix

Rule : Double the final consonant if a one-syllable word ends in a single vowel followed by a single consonant, or if a multi-syllable word has the stress on the final syllable.

Examples: run → running
- sit → sitting
- begin → beginning

## Change Y to I Before Adding a Suffix

Rule : Change "y" to "i" when adding a suffix (except when the suffix starts with "i").
Examples :
- happy → happiness
- party → parties

# Spelling Rules

## Plural of Nouns

Rule : For most nouns, add "s" to form the plural. If the noun ends in s, x, z, ch, or sh, add "es.
Examples : cat → cats, box → boxes, bus → buses

## Plural of Nouns Ending in Y

Rule : Change "y" to "ies" for nouns ending in a consonant + "y." For nouns ending in a vowel + "y," just add "s."
- Examples: city → cities, baby → babies, boy → boys

## Adding Suffixes to Words Ending in F or FE

Rule : When adding suffixes to words ending in "f" or "fe," change "f" to "v" and add "es" or "ed."
Examples : leaf → leaves , knife → knives

## Use "S" for Possessive Nouns

Rule : For singular nouns, add an apostrophe and "s" to show possession. For plural nouns ending in "s," just add an apostrophe.

Examples : Mary's book, The dogs' park

# Spelling Rules

## Spelling with Silent Letters

Rule : Certain letters in words are silent, meaning they are not pronounced but are part of the spelling.
- Examples: knee (silent "k") - talk (silent "l") - ghost (silent "h")

## Homophones and Homonyms

- Rule : Words that sound alike but have different meanings or spellings must be used correctly based on context.
- Examples: there (place) / their (possession) / they're (they are)

## Prefixes and Suffixes

- Rule : Adding prefixes or suffixes to base words can change their meaning or grammatical function. Be aware of how they affect spelling.
- Examples: un- (unhappy, undo), -ful (hopeful, careful), -ness (happiness, darkness)

## . Spellings with "C" and "G"

- Rule : "C" before e, i, or y is pronounced as /s/, and "g" before e, i, or y is pronounced as /j/.
- Examples: - cease (pronounced /s/) .- city (pronounced /s/)
- gem (pronounced /j/), - giant (pronounced /j/)

# C, ck or K?

In <u>one syllable words</u>, we use the letter 'c' before the vowels **a**, **o**, and **u**.
We use the letter '**k**' before the vowels **e** and **i**.
Use "**CK**" after a short vowel
When the /k/ sound follows a short vowel sound, use C

can
cop
cut

duck
pack
kick

Kit
Kid
Key

# Bossy r

When a vowel is followed by an "R," the "R" changes the sound of the vowel. The vowel sound is no longer long or short but takes on a unique, controlled sound.

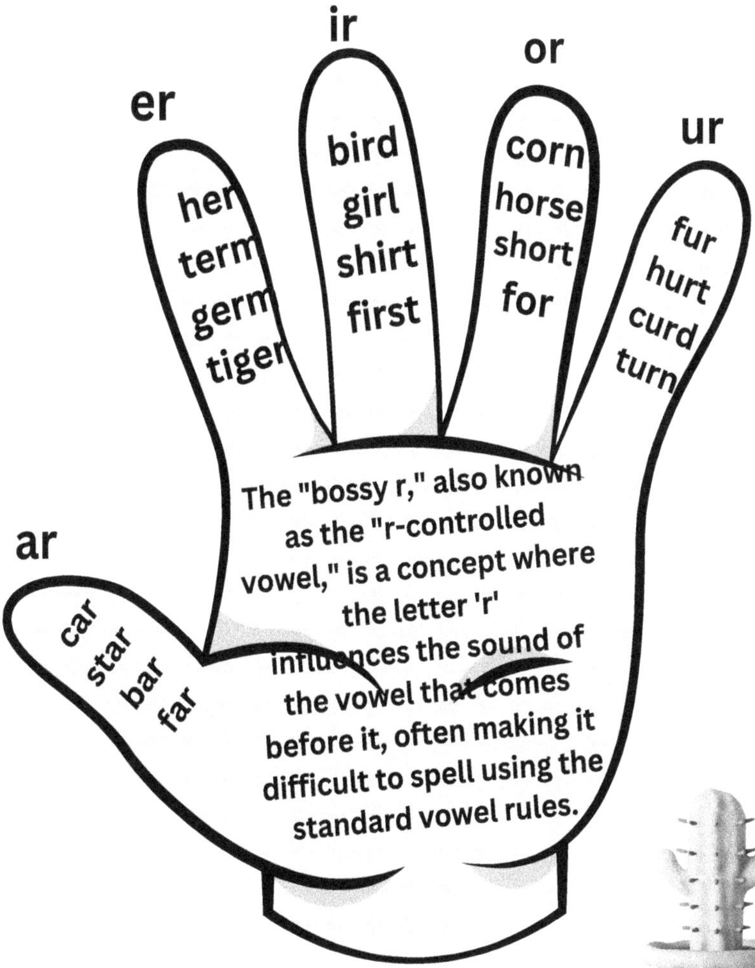

**er**: her, term, germ, tiger

**ir**: bird, girl, shirt, first

**or**: corn, horse, short, for

**ur**: fur, hurt, curd, turn

**ar**: car, star, bar, far

The "bossy r," also known as the "r-controlled vowel," is a concept where the letter 'r' influences the sound of the vowel that comes before it, often making it difficult to spell using the standard vowel rules.

# Magic E

When "E" is added at the end of a word, it is silent, but it causes the vowel in the word to "say its name" (become a long vowel sound).

### Exceptions to the Rule
While the Magic E rule applies broadly, some words (like give or love) don't follow the pattern, and the "E" does not make the vowel long.

### Examples:
- Cap **Cape** (short "A" to long "A")
- Kit **Kite** (short "I" to long "I")
- Cub **Cube** (short "U" to long "U")
- Tot **Tote** (short "O" to long "O")

## A Words:
Plan → Plane
Man → Mane
Can → Cane

## O Words:
Rob → Robe
Dot → Dote
Pop → Pope

## U Words:
Tub → Tube
Cut → Cute
Cub → Cube

## E Words:
Red → Rede (rare)
Bet → Bete (uncommon but real)
Pet → Pete

## I Words:
Rip → Ripe
Fin → Fine
Kit → Kite

## Key Points to Remember:
1. **Silent E is not pronounced.**
   - It's written but has no audible sound.
2. **It only affects the preceding vowel.**
   - The vowel before the consonant becomes long because of the silent E.
3. **Not all final E's are "Magic."**
   - In some cases, the final "E" doesn't change the vowel sound but serves other purposes (e.g., keeping "C" or "G" soft: chance, large).

# SOFT G SPELLING RULE

- The letter "g" makes a soft sound when it's followed by the vowels "e", "i", or "y". The soft "g" is pronounced as a "j" sound

- The letter "g" makes a hard sound when it's followed by other vowels or consonants, except for "y".

- A "g" at the end of a word is usually hard, as in "rag". To make a soft "g" at the end of a word, add a silent "e", as in "rage".

| HARD G | SOFT G |
|---|---|
| gate | gem |
| goat | gym |
| foggy | wage |
| gutter | age |
| glue | danger |

# Silent Letters

Silent letters are letters in words that are written but not pronounced. They often occur due to historical changes in language or borrowing from other languages. Here are the rules and common patterns for silent letters:

## Silent B

- Rule: Silent at the end of a word if it follows M.
    - Examples: comb, dumb, thumb
- Rule: Sometimes silent in other positions due to historical reasons.
    - Example: subtle

## Silent C

- Rule: Silent in the combination SC before E, I, or Y.
    - Examples: science, scene, scythe

## Silent D

- Rule: Often silent in words borrowed from other languages, especially before G.
    - Examples: Wednesday, edge

## Silent E

- Rule: Typically silent at the end of a word, serving to modify the preceding vowel.
    - Examples: cake, hope, time
- Rule: Sometimes added for etymological or spelling reasons.
    - Example: axe

## 5. Silent G

- Rule: Silent when followed by N.
    - Examples: gnaw, gnome
- Rule: Silent in some other cases, often historical.
    - Example: sign

# Silent H

- Rule: Silent in many words of French origin or after certain letters like C, G, R.
    - Examples: hour, honest, rhyme
- Rule: Silent in combinations like GH (though it affects vowel pronunciation).
    - Examples: night, thought

# Silent K

- Rule: Silent before N at the beginning of a word.
    - Examples: knight, know, knee

# Silent L

- Rule: Silent after A or O in certain words.
    - Examples: calm, folk, half

# Silent P

- Rule: Silent at the start of words followed by S, N, or T in Greek-derived terms.
    - Examples: psychology, pneumonia, pterodactyl

# Silent T

- Rule: Silent in some French-derived words or before CH.
    - Examples: ballet, catch

# Silent W

- Rule: Silent at the beginning of a word before R.
    - Examples: write, wrist
- Rule: Silent in some other contexts.
    - Example: sword

# Silent U

- Rule: Silent after G and before a vowel.
    - Examples: guess, guitar

### When to Use -tion
- Words that end in -tion are more common and usually derive from Latin words.
- Often used when the root word ends in -t or doesn't require a spelling change.

### When to Use -sion
- Words that end in -sion often follow roots that end in -s, -d, or -l.
- It's used when the root word changes slightly to accommodate the suffix.

**Examples of -tion:**
- Act → Action
- Educate → Education
- Create → Creation
- Protect → Protection
- Communicate → Communication

**Examples of -sion:**
- Decide → Decision
- Divide → Division
- Explode → Explosion
- Confuse → Confusion
- Extend → Extension

### When to Use "-tian"
- Used for words derived from Latin roots or with meanings that are more general or not profession-specific.

### When to Use "-cian"
- Specifically used for profession-related nouns, especially people skilled in certain areas.

**Examples:**
- Martian (relating to Mars).
- Christian (follower of Christianity).
- Egyptian (relating to Egypt).

**Examples:**
- Musician (skilled in music).
- Physician (medical doctor).
- Electrician (skilled in electrical work).

### When to Use -tial
Use -tial when the root word ends in -t or has a hard "t" sound before the suffix. These words often have a Latin origin.

**Examples of -tial:**
- Essential (essence → essential)
- Potential (potent → potential)
- Partial (part → partial)
- Initial (initiate → initial)
- Presidential (president → presidential)

### When to Use -cial
Use -cial when the root word ends in -c or has a soft "c" sound. These words are also frequently of Latin origin.

**Examples of -cial:**
- Special (species → special)
- Social (society → social)
- Official (office → official)
- Financial (finance → financial)
- Commercial (commerce → commercial)

### Words with -ture often relate to abstract ideas or physical structures.
**Examples**
- Nature
- Structure
- Adventure
- Future

### Words with -sure are often related to actions or conditions, such as "to measure" (verb) or "measurement" (noun).
**Examples**
- Closure
- Exposure
- Pressure
- Leisure

# The Word

Words are fundamental units of language that carry meaning. They can be classified into different types based on their functions and roles within a sentence. Here are some common types of words:

1. **Simple Words:** Simple words are basic words that cannot be broken down into smaller meaningful parts. They are usually words that represent fundamental concepts or objects.
Examples: Dog, Cat ,Book, Run, Happy

2. **Compound Words**: Compound words are formed by combining two or more simple words to create a new word with its own meaning. These words often retain the meanings of their individual parts.
Examples:
    a. Raincoat (rain + coat)
    b. Butterfly (butter + fly)
    c. Toothbrush (tooth + brush)
    d. Snowman (snow + man)
    e. Football (foot + ball)

3. **Derivative Words**: Derivative words are formed by adding prefixes or suffixes to simple words (or sometimes compound words) to change their meaning or grammatical function.
Examples:
- ·Happy (original word) -> Unhappy (prefix un- added, meaning opposite)
- ·Cook (original word) -> Cooker (suffix -er added, indicating a person or thing that does the action)
- ·Friend (original word) -> Friendship (suffix -ship added, indicating a state or condition)
- ·Love (original word) -> Lovely (suffix -ly added, changing the adjective form)

These examples should give you a good understanding of simple, compound, and derivative words.

# Capitalization Rules

1. **First Word of a Sentence**
   - Example: The cat is sleeping.
2. **Proper Nouns and Proper Adjectives**
   - Examples: Albert Einstein, New York City, Coca-Cola
   - Example: She loves Italian food.
3. **Titles**
   - Titles of People
   - Titles of Works
4. **Pronoun "I"**
   - Example: He said, "I am happy."
5. **Days, Months, and Holidays**
   - Examples: Monday, January, Christmas, spring
6. **Geographical Names**
   - Examples: Mount Everest, the Amazon River, the Pacific Ocean
7. **Events and Time Periods**
   - Examples: World War II, the Renaissance, the Great Depression
8. **Languages, Nationalities, and Religions**
   - Examples: French, Japanese, Christianity
9. **Specific Courses and Subjects**
   - Examples: Biology 101, English Literature
10. **Quotations**
    - Example: He said, "The weather is beautiful today."
11. **Letters and Abbreviations**
    - Examples: NASA, A-grade

**Common Mistakes to Avoid**

- Do not capitalize common nouns or generic terms unless part of a proper noun.
   - Incorrect: I love Summer.
   - Correct: I love summer.

# PREFIXES AND SUFFIXES

**Prefixes**: These are added to the beginning of a word and can alter its meaning or create a new word. For example, adding un- to the word happy forms unhappy, changing the meaning to not happy.:

## Common Prefixes and Examples

- **Un- (not, opposite of)**
  - Unhappy (not happy)
  - Unlock (not locked)
  - Unsafe (not safe)
- **Re- (again)**
  - Redo (do again)
  - Replay (play again)
  - Rewrite (write again)
- **Pre- (before)**
  - Preview (view before)
  - Predict (say before it happens)
  - Prepare (get ready before)
- **Dis- (not, opposite of)**
  - Dislike (not like)
  - Disconnect (not connected)
  - Dishonest (not honest)
- **Mis- (wrongly, badly)**
  - Misunderstand (understand wrongly)
  - Mistake (something done wrongly)
  - Misplace (put in the wrong place)
- **Over- (too much)**
  - Overcook (cook too much)
  - Overload (too much load)
  - Overreact (react too strongly)
- **Under- (too little, below)**
  - Undercook (cook too little)
  - Underestimate (estimate too low)
  - Underground (below the ground)
- **Non- (not)**
  - Nonsense (not making sense)
  - Nonstop (without stopping)
  - Nonfiction (not fiction)
- **In-/Im-/Ir-/Il- (not; depending the root word)**
  - Incomplete (not complete)
  - Impossible (not possible)
  - Irregular (not regular)
  - Illegal (not legal)
- **Sub- (under, below)**
  - Submarine (underwater vehicle)
  - Subtitle (text below a video)
  - Subway (train system below the ground)
- **Anti- (against)**
  - Antibiotic (fights against bacteria)
  - Antisocial (against social interaction)
  - Antifreeze (prevents freezing)
- **Co- (together, with)**
  - Cooperate (work together)
  - Coworker (someone who works with you)
  - Coexist (live together peacefully)
- **De- (opposite of, remove)**
  - Defrost (remove frost)
  - Deactivate (make inactive)
  - Decrease (go down or lessen)
- **Tri-/Bi-/Mono-/Multi- (number or amounts)**
  - Triangle (three-sided shape)
  - Bicycle (two-wheeled vehicle)
  - Monotone (one tone)
  - Multicolor (many colors)

# COMMON PREFIXES

| PREFIX | MEANING | EXAMPLES |
|---|---|---|
| anti- | against | antidote |
| de- | opposite | defrost |
| dis- | not, opposite of | disapprove |
| en- em- | cause to | encode, embrace |
| fore- | before | forecast |
| in- im- | not | incomplete, imperfect |
| il- ir- | not | illegal, irresponsible |
| inter- | between/among | interaction |
| mid- | middle | midday |
| mis- | wrongly | misunderstanding |
| non- | not | nonsense |
| over- | over | overreaction |
| pre- | before | predetermined |
| re- | again | rearrange |
| semi- | half | semicircle |
| sub- | under | submarine |
| super- | above | superiority |
| trans- | across | transform |
| un- | not | unkind |
| under- | under | underdeveloped |

# Suffixes:

These are added to the end of a word and can change its grammatical function, tense, or meaning. For instance, adding -ed to the verb talk forms talked, indicating past tense

## Common Suffixes and Examples
- **-ed (past tense)**
  - Played (past of play)
  - Jumped (past of jump)
  - Walked (past of walk)
- **-ing (present participle/continuous action)**
  - Running (action of run)
  - Swimming (action of swim)
  - Reading (action of read)
- **-s / -es (plural or third person singular)**
  - Dogs (more than one dog)
  - Watches (more than one watch)
  - Runs (he/she runs)
- **-er (one who, comparative)**
  - Teacher (one who teaches)
  - Runner (one who runs)
  - Faster (more fast)
- **-est (superlative)**
  - Tallest (most tall)
  - Smartest (most smart)
  - Fastest (most fast)
- **-ly (in what manner, adverb)**
  - Quickly (in a quick manner)
  - Happily (in a happy manner)
  - Slowly (in a slow manner)
- **-ness (state or quality, noun)**
  - Kindness (the quality of being kind)
  - Happiness (the state of being happy)
  - Sadness (the state of being sad)
- **-ful (full of, adjective)**
  - Hopeful (full of hope)
  - Joyful (full of joy)
  - Helpful (full of help)
- **-less (without, adjective)**
  - Hopeless (without hope)
  - Careless (without care)
  - Fearless (without fear)
- **-able / -ible (can be done, adjective)**
  - Washable (can be washed)
  - Breakable (can be broken)
  - Edible (can be eaten)
- **-ment (action or result, noun)**
  - Payment (result of paying)
  - Development (process of developing)
  - Achievement (result of achieving)
- **-tion / -sion (state or action, noun)**
  - Celebration (act of celebrating)
  - Decision (act of deciding)
  - Education (process of educating)
- **-y (characterized by, adjective)**
  - Sunny (full of sun)
  - Funny (causing laughter)
  - Messy (full of mess)
- **-ous / -ious / -eous (full of, adjective)**
  - Dangerous (full of danger)
  - Famous (full of fame)
  - Curious (full of curiosity)
- **-ist (one who, noun)**
  - Artist (one who creates art)
  - Scientist (one who practices science)
  - Pianist (one who plays the piano)

# COMMON SUFFIXES

| SUFFIX | MEANING | EXAMPLES |
|---|---|---|
| -able -ible | able to be | suitable, visible |
| -al -ial | having characteristics of | personal, influential |
| -ed | past-tense verb | skipped |
| -en | made of | wooden |
| -er | comparative | older |
| -er | one who | carpenter |
| -est | comparative | biggest |
| -ful | full of | beautiful |
| -ic | having characteristics of | iconic |
| -ing | present participle verb | shopping |
| -ion -tion | act, process | occasion, attraction |
| -ation -ition | act, process | starvation, contrition |
| -ity -ty | state of | scarcity, cruelty |
| -ive -ative -itive | adjective form of a noun | destructive, initiative, fugitive |
| -less | without | careless |
| -ly | characteristic of | quickly |
| -ment | action or process | achievement |
| -ness | state of, condition of | Forgiveness |
| -ous -eous -ious | possessing the qualities of | famous, courteous, suspicious |
| -s -es | more than one | shoes, dresses |
| -y | characterised by | dirty |

# SYLLABLES

**Syllables** are the building blocks of words, each containing a single vowel sound, or a vowel sound with consonants before or after it. Here's a breakdown:

1. **Definition** : A syllable is a unit of sound in a word, typically containing a vowel, and sometimes one or more consonants.

2. **Types of Syllables** :
   - **Open Syllable** : Ends with a vowel sound, e.g., no or hi.
   - **Closed Syllable** : Ends with a consonant sound, e.g., cat or sandwich
   - **Vowel-Consonant-e Syllable** : Contains a vowel followed by a consonant and a silent e at the end, e.g., cake or hope.
   - **Consonant-le Syllable** : Contains a consonant followed by -le at the end, e.g., table or bubble.
   - **R-Controlled Syllable** : Contains a vowel followed by the letter r, e.g., car or bird.
   - **Diphthong** : A single syllable containing two vowel sounds, e.g., coin or noise.

3. **Counting Syllables** : You can count syllables by pronouncing the word slowly and noting each separate vowel sound.

4. **Importance**: Understanding syllables helps with pronunciation, spelling, and reading fluency. It's particularly crucial for early literacy development in children.

5. **Syllable Division Rules** :
   - **VC/CV Rule** : Divide between two consonants in the middle of a word, e.g., hap-py or din-ner.
   - **V/V Rule** : If two vowels are together but represent separate sounds, divide between them, e.g., li-on or pi-an-o.
   - **VC/V Rule** : If there's a consonant followed by a vowel, divide after the consonant, e.g., sud-den or hop-ing.
   - **VCCV Rule** : When there are two consonants between two vowels, divide between them, e.g., butter or rabbit.

6. **Role in Poetry**: Syllables are crucial in poetry for meter and rhythm. Different poetic forms have specific syllable patterns, like haiku (5-7-5 syllable structure).

7. **Languages with Complex Syllable Structures** : Some languages have more complex syllable structures than English, such as Japanese or Hawaiian, where each syllable consists of a consonant followed by a vowel.

Understanding syllables aids in pronunciation, spelling, and reading comprehension, making it an essential aspect of language learning and literacy.

# What's the Rule?

## When to use double letters

Use double letters when:
- A word has one syllable.
- There is a short vowel before the consonant.

| Word | One Syllable? | | Short Vowel before the Consonant? | What's the Word? |
|---|---|---|---|---|
| clap | Yes | | Yes | clapping |
| sit | Yes | | Yes | sitting |
| jump | Yes | | No | jumping |
| grab | Yes | | Yes | grabbing |
| point | Yes | | No | pointing |

Here are some examples of words with different syllable counts:

### 1 Syllable Words (1 beat)

- Cat
- Dog
- Sun
- Tree
- Jump

### 2 Syllable Words (2 beats)

- Water (wa-ter)
- Table (ta-ble)
- Happy (hap-py)
- Winter (win-ter)
- Flower (flow-er)

### 3 Syllable Words (3 beats)

- Banana (ba-na-na)
- Family (fam-i-ly)
- Elephant (el-e-phant)
- Adventure (ad-ven-ture)
- Chocolate (choc-o-late)

### 4 Syllable Words (4 beats)

- Banana (ba-na-na)
- Family (fam-i-ly)
- Elephant (el-e-phant)
- Adventure (ad-ven-ture)
- Chocolate (choc-o-late)

### 5 or more Syllable Words (5 or more beats)

- Responsibility (re-spon-si-bil-i-ty)
- Unbelievable (un-be-liev-a-ble)
- Communication (com-mu-ni-ca-tion)

You can clap along to the word to help identify the syllables or use your hand to feel the chin drop for each vowel sound.

# THE ARTICLES

In English grammar, articles are words used to specify or indicate whether a noun refers to a specific or general entity. There are three articles: **the**, **a**, and **an**. The is the definite article, used before specific nouns that the speaker and listener both know about or can identify in context. A and an are indefinite articles, used before non-specific or generic nouns. A is used before words that begin with consonant sounds, while an is used before words that begin with vowel sounds. Articles help provide clarity and specificity in sentences.

here's a detailed breakdown of the articles a, an, and the :

1. **A and An (Indefinite Articles):**
   - **Usage**: Both a and an are indefinite articles used before singular nouns to indicate that the noun refers to any member of a group.
   - **Selection**: A is used before words that begin with a consonant sound, while an is used before words that begin with a vowel sound.
   - Examples:
     - A car (the noun car starts with a consonant sound)
     - An apple (the noun apple starts with a vowel sound)
     - Note: The choice between a and an is based on the sound of the following word, not necessarily its spelling.

2. **The (Definite Article):**
   - **Usage**: The is a definite article used before singular or plural nouns to indicate that the noun refers to a specific entity or entities.
   - **Specificity**: It indicates that the noun being referred to is already known to the reader or listener, or that it is unique or specific within the context.
   - Examples:
     1. The car parked outside is mine. (referring to a specific car)
     2. Please pass the salt. (referring to a specific object, salt)
   - **Function**: The can also be used to indicate that the noun being referred to is unique in the context or that it is a particular member of a group.
   - Examples:
     - The sun rises in the east. (referring to the specific star that is central to Earth's solar system)
     - The President of the United States (referring to a specific individual holding the position)

# Articles: A, An or The
# Answer Key

### A. Fill in the blanks

1. We went to **a** concert last night.
2. Can you pass me **the** salt, please?
3. **The** tallest mountain in the world is Mount Everest.
4. I need to buy **a** new pair of shoes.
5. **The** Mona Lisa is a famous painting by Leonardo da Vinci.
6. London is **the** capital of England.
7. I saw **an** interesting movie yesterday, but I can't remember **the** title.
8. **The** sun is a star, and **The** Earth revolves around it.
9. **The** Great Wall of China is one of the Seven Wonders of the Ancient World.
10. Please turn on **the** light in the kitchen.
11. We need **a** compass to find ___ north.
12. Did you see **a** butterfly in the garden?
13. **The** Eiffel Tower is a famous landmark in Paris.
14. I'm learning to play **the** piano.
15. Please pass me **a** napkin, please.
16. **The** Mississippi River is a major river in the United States.
17. **The** internet has changed the way we communicate.
18. We went to **the** zoo and saw lions and tigers.

### B. Circle the best article.

1. Please close **the** curtains, the sun is too bright.
2. Did you see **a** butterfly in the garden yesterday?
3. **The** Amazon rainforest is home to many different animals.
4. I'm learning to play **the** piano, it's a lot of fun!
5. Would you like **a** cup of tea?
6. Would you like to see **the** picture I drew yesterday?
7. **The** milk has gone bad, we need to buy **a** new one.
8. Can you hand me **a/an** tissue, please? I have a runny nose.
9. There's **an** apple tree in **the** backyard.
10. **The** Statue of Liberty is a symbol of freedom.
11. We need **a** map to find the nearest bus stop.
12. There's **an** interesting article about dinosaurs in this magazine.
13. Paris is known as **the** City of Lights.
14. We need **an** appointment with the dentist to get our teeth checked.
15. I saw **a** red car parked outside my window.
16. Please turn down **the** volume on the TV, it's too loud.
17. Learning **an** instrument can be a rewarding experience.
18. My mother is **an** excellent baker, her pies are delicious!

# THE SENTENCE

1. **Definition**: A sentence is a grammatical unit of language that typically expresses a complete thought. It consists of a subject and a predicate, with the subject usually indicating who or what the sentence is about, and the predicate providing information about the subject. Sentences can vary in length and complexity and can convey different types of information..

2. **Parts of a Sentence** :
   - **Subject** : The part of the sentence that performs the action or about which something is said.
   - **Predicate** : The part of the sentence that contains the verb and provides information about the subject.
   - Object : If present, the object receives the action of the verb.

3. **Types of Sentences** :
   - **Affirmative Sentences**: An affirmative sentence is a sentence that states something positively, asserts a fact, or expresses agreement. In English, affirmative sentences typically follow the subject-verb-object order, where the subject is doing something or being something.

Examples of affirmative sentences:
- She sings beautifully.
- They are going to the party tonight.
- The sun rises in the east.
- He likes chocolate ice cream.
- We are learning about history in school.

In each of these examples, the sentences express something that is true or happening in a positive manner.

- **Negative Sentences**: A negative sentence, on the other hand, is a sentence that negates or denies something. It expresses the absence or lack of something, or it contradicts a positive statement. In English, negative sentences typically use the auxiliary verb do (in various forms) along with not or other negative words to form the negative.

Examples of negative sentences:
- She does not sing very well.
- They are not going to the party tonight.
- The sun does not rise in the west.
- He does not like chocolate ice cream.
- We are not studying math today.

- **Assertive sentences**, also known as declarative sentences, are statements that provide information or make assertions. They can express facts, opinions, beliefs, or observations. Assertive sentences typically end with a period. Here are some examples of assertive sentences:
1. The sun rises in the east.
·This sentence states a fact about the direction of the sunrise.
2. I believe that education is the key to success.
·Here, the speaker expresses their opinion about the importance of education.
3. She is a talented musician.
·This sentence makes an assertion about someone's talent in music.
4. The Earth revolves around the sun.
·Another factual statement about the movement of celestial bodies.
5. He seems upset about something.
·This sentence expresses an observation about someone's emotional state.

- **Interrogative sentences** are sentences that ask a question or seek information. They are typically characterized by their use of question words (such as who, what, where, when, why, how) or by their use of auxiliary verbs (like is, are, can, do, have) to form questions. Interrogative sentences usually end with a question mark. Here are some examples:
1. What time is the meeting?
·This sentence asks for information about the time of the meeting.
2. Where did you go on vacation?
·Here, the speaker seeks information about the destination of the listener's vacation.
3. Who is coming to the party?
·This question asks about the identities of the attendees at the party.
4. Why are you upset?
·The speaker wants to know the reason behind the listener's emotional state.
5. How do you solve this equation?
·This question seeks information about the method for solving a mathematical equation.
6. Can you help me with my homework?
·Here, the speaker asks for assistance with homework.
7. Did you finish your assignment?
·This interrogative sentence asks whether the listener completed a task.
Interrogative sentences are used to gather information, seek clarification, initiate conversations, and engage others in dialogue. They prompt the listener to respond with answers or explanations.

- **Imperative sentences** are sentences that give commands, instructions, or make requests. They are used to direct someone to do something or to instruct them on how to do it. Imperative sentences often end with a period (.) but can also end with an exclamation mark (!) if the command is urgent or forceful.

Here are some examples of imperative sentences:
1. Close the door, please.
2. Brush your teeth before bed.
3. Sit down and be quiet.
4. Please pass the salt.
5. Don't touch that!

In each of these examples, the speaker is giving a command, instruction, or making a request to someone else. Imperative sentences are straightforward and direct in conveying what needs to be done.

- **Exclamatory sentences** are used to express strong emotions such as excitement, surprise, anger, or admiration. They often end with an exclamation mark (!) to convey the heightened emotion. These sentences can be statements or commands, but they are distinguished by the intense feeling they convey. Here are some examples:
1. What a beautiful sunset!
2. I can't believe we won the lottery!
3. Wow, that was an incredible performance!
4. How dare you speak to me like that!
5. Congratulations on your promotion!

In each of these examples, the exclamation mark emphasizes the emotion being expressed, whether it's joy, surprise, pain, or urgency.

- **An operative sentence**, also known as a declarative sentence, is a type of sentence that makes a statement or expresses an idea. It typically ends with a period. Here are a few examples of operative sentences:
1. The sun rises in the east. - This sentence states a fact.
2. She painted the walls blue. - This sentence describes an action performed by someone.
3. The cat is sleeping on the couch. - This sentence provides information about the current state of the cat.
4. John loves to read books. - This sentence expresses a person's preference or habit.
5. The concert begins at 7 PM. - This sentence communicates an event's time.

In each example, the operative sentence conveys a clear message or idea.
Top of Form

# SENTENCE TYPES
## BY STRUCTURE

### SIMPLE

A simple sentence has one independent clause. No commas seperate two compound elements in a simple sentence.

*E.g. Anna eats lollies.*

### COMPOUND

A compound sentence has two independent clauses joined by a coordinating conjunction (e.g. for, and, nor, but, or, yet, so), a conjunctive adverb (e.g. however, therefore) or a semicolon.

*E.g. Anna eats lollies but Jamie eats fruit.*

### COMPLEX

A complex sentence has one dependent clause (headed by a subordinating conjunction or a relative pronoun) joined to an independent clause.

*E.g. Although Anna eats lollies, Jamie eats fruit.*

### COMPOUND COMPLEX

A compound-complex sentence has two independent clauses joined to one or more dependent clauses.

# PUNCTUATION

**QUESTION MARK** — Use at the end of a sentence when asking a question.

**EXCLAMATION MARK** — Use at the end of a sentence to express a strong feeling.

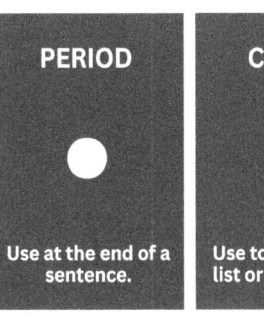
**PERIOD** — Use at the end of a sentence.

**COLON** — Use to introduce a list or a definition.

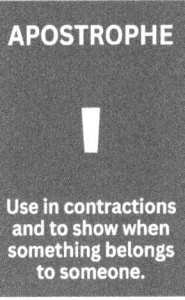
**APOSTROPHE** — Use in contractions and to show when something belongs to someone.

**PARENTHESIS** — Use to add extra information to a sentence without taking away from the idea.

**HYPHEN** — Use to join separate words to make one word.

**SEMICOLON** — Use to connect subjects and verbs into a single sentence.

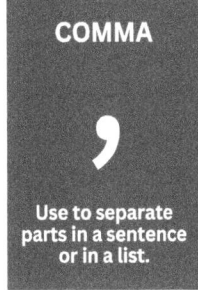
**COMMA** — Use to separate parts in a sentence or in a list.

**QUOTATIONS** — Use around words that are spoken.

**ELLIPSIS** — Use to show suspense or that someone is thinking.

# Punctuation in Sentences

Punctuation plays a crucial role in sentences by providing structure, clarity, and meaning to written language. Here are some key punctuation marks and their functions in sentences:

1. **Period (.)**: The period is used to indicate the end of a declarative sentence, which makes a statement or expresses an idea.
·Example:   She enjoys reading books.
2. **Question Mark (?)**: The question mark is used at the end of interrogative sentences, which ask questions.
·Example:   What time is the meeting?
3. **Exclamation Mark (!)**: The exclamation mark is used at the end of exclamatory sentences, which express strong emotions or exclamations.
·Example:   Wow, what a beautiful sunset!
4. **Comma (,)**: Commas have various functions, including separating items in a list, separating clauses in compound sentences, setting off introductory phrases or clauses, and indicating pauses in a sentence.
·Example:   She likes apples, oranges, and bananas.
5.**Semicolon (;)**: Semicolons are used to connect closely related independent clauses in a sentence.
·Example:   She finished her work; then she went for a walk.
6. **Colon (:)**: Colons are used to introduce lists, explanations, quotations, or to indicate a ratio.
·Example:   Please bring the following items: bread, milk, and eggs.
7. **Dash (–)**: Dashes are used to indicate a sudden change in thought, set off additional information within a sentence, or emphasize a point.
·Example:   She bought flowers – roses, tulips, and daisies – for the party.
8. **Quotation Marks ( " )**: Quotation marks are used to enclose direct speech, dialogue, or quotations.
·Example: She said,   I'll see you tomorrow.
9.   **Parentheses (())**: Parentheses are used to set off additional information within a sentence, such as clarifications, asides, or citations.
·Example:   The event (which was held last week) was a great success.
9.   **Sentence Clarity**: Clear sentences are essential for effective communication. Avoiding ambiguity, using concise language, and ensuring proper grammar and punctuation contribute to clarity.
10. **Sentence Variety**: Varying sentence structure and length adds interest and rhythm to writing, making it more engaging for readers.

# PARTS OF SPEECH

The role a word plays in a sentence.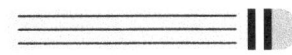

## NOUN

✓ A noun is a person, place, thing, idea, or concept.

**Examples:** country, doctor, happiness, vehicle, cat, history, sister, music, chocolate, avalanche, pride
The <u>girl</u> felt immense <u>pride</u> after receiving a high <u>grade</u> on her <u>test</u>.

## PRONOUN

✓ Pronouns replace a noun to avoid repetition.

**Examples:** she, he, they, them, it, us, we, our, themselves, ourselves, mine, their, you
Eleanor loves ice cream. <u>Her</u> favorite flavor is cookie dough.

## VERB

✓ Verbs represent internal and external actions or states of being.

**Examples:** dance, sing, sleep, crouch, tip toe, is scream, cook, am, were, had, being, can, would
The waiter <u>was startled</u> by the dishes <u>crashing</u> to the floor.

## ADVERB

✓ Adverbs modify a verb, adjective, or another adverb.

**Examples:** always, very, quickly, proudly, neatly, accordingly, lately, sometimes
He <u>rarely</u> left the library without <u>at least</u> two new books.

## ADJECTIVE

✓ Adjectives describe or modify nouns or pronouns

**Examples:** creative, polite, gentle, nice, absurd, odd friendly, bittersweet

Although the math test was <u>challenging</u>, he was happy with his grade.

## PREPOSITION

✓ Prepositions show a relationship between words

**Examples:** on, inside, before, under, beneath, above, against, below, within

Tomorrow, she will ride her bike <u>down</u> the street and <u>through</u> the park <u>in</u> a race.

## INTERJECTION

✓ Interjections express a strong emotion, feeling, or exclamation

**Examples:** wow, ouch, whoa, hey, um, ahem, yikes, oh my gosh

"<u>Whoa</u>! Did you see that lightning?" he exclaimed.

## CONJUNCTION

✓ Conjunctions join words, phrases, and clauses to show a connection

**Examples:** for, and, nor, but, or, yet, so, whether, neither, because

Not only is the weather humid, <u>but</u> it is also rainy and foggy.

This is a fun, rhyming poem that explains the eight basic parts of speech. The first line of each stanza explain what each part of speech does.

Every name is called a **noun**,
As field and fountain, street and town.
In place of noun the **pronoun** stands,
As he and she can clap their hands.
The **adjective** describes a thing,
As magic wand or bridal ring.
The **verb** means action, something done,
To read and write, to jump and run.
How things are done the **adverbs** tell,
As quickly, slowly, badly, well.
The **preposition** shows relation,
As in the street or at the station.
**Conjunctions** join, in many ways,
Sentences, words, or phrase and phrase.
The **interjection** cries out, Hark!
I need an exclamation mark!

Through poetry, we learn how each of these make up the PARTS OF SPEECH.

# NOUN

A noun is a word that names something, such a person, place, thing or idea. In a sentence, nouns can play the role of subject, direct object, indirect object, subject complement, object complement or adjective. There are different types of nouns:

### Proper nouns

Nouns that are used to name a person, place or thing specifically are called a proper noun. Proper nouns always begin with a capital letter.

### Common nouns

They refer to a generic item, group or place. This means that, unlike proper nouns, they are not used to identify specific people, places or objects.

### Singular nouns

These are words that are used to name a single person, place, animal, bird or object.

### Plural nouns

Plural nouns refer to a number of people, places, animals or things. Nouns are made plural by adding an 's' or 'es' or 'ies' or 'ves' to the existing root word.

### Countable nouns

Nouns that can be counted or measured.

### Uncountable nouns

They are those nouns that cannot be counted. This category of nouns includes both concrete and abstract nouns.

### Concrete nouns

A concrete noun refers to objects that are material and can be perceived by the human senses.

### Abstract nouns

Any entity that cannot be perceived by the five senses of the human body are called an abstract noun.

### Collective nouns

A collective noun is a naming word that is used to denote a group of objects, animals or people.

# NOUN

A noun is a word that refers to a person (Mary), a thing (pen), an animal (cat), a place (Bangalore), a quality (kindness).

| SL | Types Of Nouns | Definition | Examples |
|---|---|---|---|
| 1. | Concrete Noun | A concrete noun is a noun that refers to a physical thing, person, or place—something or someone that can be perceived with the five senses (touch, hearing, sight, smell, and taste). | Name of a person, place, thing, animals, sports, games etc., |
| 1.1 | Proper noun | A proper noun is the name of a particular person, place, organization, or thing and it begins with capital letter. | Siyara, Bangalore, Pencil, Tiger, Hockey, etc., |
| 1.2 | Common Noun | A common Noun is a name given to any person, place, or thing in general. | Girl, boy, doctor, officer, etc., |
| 1.3 | Collective noun | A collective noun is a noun that refers to some sort of group or collective—of people, animals, things, etc. | Bunch, crowd, class, team etc., |
| 1.4 | Material Noun | Material Nouns are the names of the materials or substances that are used to produce products. | Cotton, metal, gold, water, rubber, wood etc., |
| 1.5 | Abstract Nouns | An abstract noun is a noun that refers to something non-physical—something conceptual that you can't perceive directly with your senses. | Quality, action, certain stage, things, (childhood, sad, joy, feelings) etc. |

# NOUN: GENDERS:

Noun classes or noun genders. These classifications are not necessarily based on biological sex but rather on grammatical rules and conventions within the language. Different languages have different systems for categorizing nouns into genders, and not all languages have gendered nouns.

Here's a brief overview of how gendered nouns might work in a hypothetical language:

**1.Masculine Gender**: Nouns that represent male beings or objects often fall into the masculine gender. For example, words like man, boy, king, father, and brother might be classified as masculine nouns.

**2.Feminine Gender**: Nouns representing female beings or objects could be categorized as feminine gender. Examples include woman, girl, queen, mother, and sister.

**3.Neuter Gender**: Some languages have a third gender category known as neuter, which typically includes inanimate objects, abstract concepts, or entities without a clear gender. Examples might include table, chair, house, love, happiness, etc.

**4.Common Gender**: In some languages, there might be a common gender category that encompasses both masculine and feminine genders. Nouns in this category can refer to beings of either sex. For instance, friend, teacher, doctor, parent, etc., might belong to the common gender.

It's important to note that gender in language doesn't always correspond to biological gender or societal gender roles. It's a grammatical feature that helps determine the form of associated words, such as articles, adjectives, and pronouns. Additionally, the specific genders and rules for categorizing nouns can vary significantly from one language to another.

# Examples of Masculine and Feminine Gender Nouns

**Masculine Gender Nouns**
1. Man
2. Father
3. Brother
4. King
5. Actor
6. Prince
7. Boy
8. Husband
9. Uncle
10. Nephew
11. Lion
12. Tiger
13. Rooster
14. Bull
15. Monk
16. Gentleman
17. Wizard
18. Drake (male duck)
19. Stallion
20. Baron
21. Peacock
22. God
23. Hero
24. Policeman
25. Waiter
26. Bachelor
27. Sir
28. Landlord
29. Count
30. Emperor

**Feminine Gender Nouns**
1. Woman
2. Mother
3. Sister
4. Queen
5. Actress
6. Princess
7. Girl
8. Wife
9. Aunt
10. Niece
11. Lioness
12. Tigress
13. Hen
14. Cow
15. Nun
16. Lady
17. Witch
18. Duck (female duck)
19. Mare
20. Baroness
21. Peahen
22. Goddess
23. Heroine
24. Policewoman
25. Waitress
26. Spinster
27. Madam
28. Landlady
29. Countess
30. Empress

# Noun; Numbers;

Number nouns, also known as count nouns or countable nouns, are nouns that can be counted and pluralized. These nouns refer to individual entities or items that can be quantified as discrete units. Examples of count nouns include:

- **Singular Nouns**: Referring to one individual entity.

·Cat, Book, Chair, Table
- **Plural Nouns**: Referring to multiple individual entities.

·Cats, Books, Chairs, Tables

Count nouns can be preceded by numerical quantifiers (such as one, two, three, etc.) or other determiners that indicate quantity (such as some, many, a few, several, etc.). They also take plural forms when there is more than one of the entity being referred to.

It's important to note that count nouns can be contrasted with non-count nouns (mass nouns), which refer to substances, concepts, or qualities that cannot be counted as individual units.

Examples of non-count nouns include water, music, happiness, and information.

1.**Counting Nouns**: Numbers can be used to count individual items or entities. For example:
- There are three apples on the table.
- She has two cats.
- There were five students in the classroom.

2.**Quantifying Nouns**: Numbers can also be used to quantify or measure nouns that are not easily counted individually. For example:
- There's a lot of traffic on the road.
- He drank too much water.
- She has a little patience.

**Summary**:
- Counting nouns involve numbers or specific items (e.g., three apples).
- Quantifying nouns specify amounts of uncountable or collective items (e.g., a loaf of bread).

3. **Ordinal Numbers**: Ordinal numbers indicate the position or order of something in a sequence. For example:
- · He finished in first place.
- · This is the third time I've told you.
- She's the second oldest in her family.

4. **Plural Nouns**: Plural nouns indicate more than one of something. While not always accompanied by a specific number, they imply a quantity greater than one. For example:
- · There are many books on the shelf.
- · Several people attended the meeting.
- · They bought some groceries at the store.

5. **Fractional Nouns**: Numbers can be used with nouns to indicate a fraction or a portion of something. For example:
- · He ate half of the pizza.
- · She drank a quarter of the bottle.
- · They spent three-quarters of their savings on the trip.

Using numbers with nouns helps provide clarity and specificity in communication, allowing us to convey precise quantities, order, or proportions

**Summary**:
1. Ordinal Numbers: Represent the rank or position in a sequence (e.g., first, second, third).
2. Plural Nouns: Represent more than one item, usually by adding -s, -es, or changing forms (e.g., cats, boxes, children).
3. Fractional Nouns: Represent parts of a whole or division into equal parts (e.g., half, one-third, two-fifths).

# Noun; cases

Cases in grammar refer to the inflectional forms of nouns, pronouns, and adjectives in some languages. They indicate the role that the word plays in the sentence, such as subject, object, possessor, etc. Different languages have different numbers and types of cases.

1.**Nominative Case:** This case is used for the subject of a sentence. It typically answers the question who? or what? For example, in the sentence The dog barks, dog is in the nominative case.

2.**Accusative Case**: This case is used for the direct object of a sentence. It generally answers the question whom? or what? For instance, in the sentence She sees the cat, cat is in the accusative case.

3.**Genitive Case:** This case indicates possession or association. It answers the question whose? For example, in the phrase The car of my brother, brother is in the genitive case.

4.**Dative Case**: This case typically indicates the indirect object of a sentence. It answers the question to/for whom? or to/for what? For instance, in the sentence I gave a book to her, her is in the dative case.

5.**Vocative Case**: This case is used for direct address or calling someone. It's used when directly addressing someone or something. For example, in the sentence Hello, John! , John would be in the vocative case.

6.**Instrumental Case**: This case often indicates the instrument or means by which an action is performed. It answers the question by what? or with what? For instance, in the sentence He wrote with a pen, pen would be in the instrumental case.

7.**Locative Case**: This case indicates a location or place where something happens. It answers the question where? For example, in the sentence The party is at Maria's house, Maria's house would be in the locative case.

# Noun; Gerund

A Gerund is a type of verbal, which means it's a word that's based on a verb but functions as a different part of speech. Specifically, a gerund functions as a noun.

Here's how a gerund works:

1. **Formation:** A gerund is formed by adding -ing to the base form of a verb. For example, the gerund form of read is reading, and the gerund form of dance is dancing.

2. **Function as a noun:** Gerunds can function in sentences as nouns, meaning they can serve as subjects, objects, or complements. They can also be used as the object of prepositions.
·**Subject**:   Reading enhances knowledge.
·**Object**:   She enjoys reading.
·**Complement**:   Her hobby is reading.
·**Object of preposition:**   He is interested in reading.

3. **Usage**: Gerunds can be used to express actions, activities, or states as nouns. They often represent activities in a general sense rather than specific instances.
Here are a few more examples:
- · Swimming is her favorite sport.  (subject)
- · I love cooking.  (object)
- · His passion is painting.  (complement)
- · She is good at singing.  (object of preposition)

In each of these sentences, the gerund form of the verb ( swimming, cooking,   painting,    singing) acts as a noun, performing the role typically associated with nouns in the sentence structure.

# PRONOUN

A pronoun is a word that is used instead of a noun or noun phrase. Pronouns are commonly used in writing and speech to avoid repetitive use of nouns, especially when referring to the same person, thing, or idea multiple times within a sentence or a paragraph. Pronouns help to make sentences clearer, more concise, and easier to understand.

## TYPES OF PRONOUNS

*Pronoun: takes the place of a noun or another pronoun*

| Type of Pronoun | Definition | Examples |
|---|---|---|
| Personal Pronouns | Refer to specific people or things | I, you, he, she, it, we, they |
| Demonstrative Pronouns | Point our specific people or things | that, this, these, those |
| Interrogative Pronouns | Used to ask questions | who, whom, whose, which, what |
| Possessive Pronouns | Show ownership or possession | mine, yours, his, hers, its, ours, theirs |
| Reflexive Pronouns | Reflect or refer back to the subject of a sentence | myself, yourself, himself, herself, itself, ourselves, themselves, yourselves |
| Intensive Pronouns | Emphasize a noun or pronoun in a sentence | myself, yourself, himself, herself, itself, ourselves, themselves, yourselves |
| Relative Pronouns | Introduce relative clauses and connect them to the noun they modify | who, whom, whose, which, that |
| Indefinite Pronouns | Refer to nonspecific people or things | all, both, many, none, few, some, anyone, several, nobody |

# Types of Pronouns;

1. **Personal pronoun**s are words used to replace or refer to specific people or things. Here are examples of personal pronouns:

1. **First Person Singular: Referring to oneself.**
   - ·I (subject):   I am going to the store.
   - ·Me (object):   John gave the book to me.

2. **Second Person Singular: Referring to the person being spoken to.**
   - ·You (subject/object):   You are my best friend.

3. **Third Person Singular: Referring to someone or something else.**
   - ·He (subject):   He is a doctor.
   - ·She (subject):   She is my sister.
   - ·It (subject/object):   The cat is sleeping. It is tired.

4. **First Person Plural: Referring to a group including oneself.**
   - ·We (subject):   We are going to the party.
   - ·Us (object):   Please join us for dinner.

5. **Second Person Plural: Referring to a group of people being spoken to.**
   - ·You (subject/object):   Are you all coming to the meeting?

6. **Third Person Plural: Referring to a group of people or things.**
   - ·They (subject):   They are studying for the exam.
   - ·Them (object):   I saw them at the park.

# PERSONAL PRONOUNS

|  | Subject Pronoun | Object pronouns | Possessive adjectives | Possessive pronouns | Reflexive pronouns |
|---|---|---|---|---|---|
| 1st person singular | I | me | my | mine | myself |
| 1st person plural | we | us | our | ours | Ourselves |
| 2nd person singular | you | you | your | yours | Yourself |
| 2nd person plural | you | you | your | yours | Yourselves |
| 3rd person | It | it | its | its | itself |
| 3rd person (female) | she | her | her | hers | Herself |
| 3rd person (male) | He | Him | his | his | himself |
| 3rd person plural | They | them | their | theirs | themselves |

2. **Interrogative pronouns** are used to ask questions and gather information about people or things. They include:
1. **Who**: Used to inquire about people.
·Example:   Who is coming to the party?
2.**Whom**: Also used to inquire about people, often in formal or written English.
·Example:   Whom did you speak to on the phone?
3. **What**: Used to inquire about things or actions.
·Example:   What is your favorite color?
4. **Which**: Used to inquire about a specific choice or selection.
·Example:   Which book did you borrow from the library?
5. **Whose**: Used to inquire about possession or ownership.
·Example:   Whose car is parked outside?
6.**Whichever**: Used to inquire about any one out of a number of choices.
·Example:   Whichever route you take, make sure to drive safely.
These pronouns are called interrogative because they are used to form questions and elicit information.

3. **Possessive pronouns indicate ownership or possession. Here are some examples of possessive pronouns:**
1.  **My**: This is my book.
2.  **Your**: Is this your phone?
3.  **His**: That is his car.
4.  **Her**: I saw her dog in the park.
5.  **Its**: The cat licked its paw.
6.  **Our**: We painted our house last summer.
7.  **There**: They brought their children to the party.
8.  **Mine**: The red pen is mine.
9.  **Yours**: Is this yours or mine?
10. **His**: His idea was brilliant.
11. **Hers**: The blue sweater is hers.
12. **Ours**: The garden is ours to maintain.
13. **Theirs**: The decision is theirs to make.
These pronouns are used to show that something belongs to or is associated with someone or something. They replace nouns to avoid repetition and make sentences clearer and more concise.

4.**Demonstrative pronouns** are used to point to specific things or people within a conversation. They can indicate proximity in space or time. In English, the main demonstrative pronouns are this, that, these, and those.

Here are some examples :
1. **This**: Used to refer to a singular noun that is close in space or time.
- This book is interesting.
- I want to buy this shirt.
2. **That**: Used to refer to a singular noun that is farther away in space or time.
- That movie was amazing.
- Look at that beautiful sunset!
3. **These**: Used to refer to plural nouns that are close in space or time.
- These cookies are delicious.
- Can you help me with these bags?
4. **Those**: Used to refer to plural nouns that are farther away in space or time.
- Those flowers are so pretty.
- I haven't seen those friends in years.

5. **Relative pronouns** are used to introduce relative clauses, which provide additional information about a noun in a sentence. Some common relative pronouns include who, whom, whose, which, and that.

Here are some examples :

1. **Who**: Used to refer to people.
- The man who is standing over there is my uncle.
- She is the doctor who treated my mother.
2. **Whom**: Also used to refer to people, particularly in formal English and as the object of a verb or preposition.
- The person whom you met yesterday is my boss.
- To whom did you send the email?
3. **Whose**: Indicates possession and is used to show ownership.
- The car, whose headlights were broken, belonged to my neighbor.
- The student, whose grades have improved, received an award.
4. **Which**: Generally used to refer to animals or things.
- The book, which is on the table, is mine.
- This is the dress which I wore to the party.
5. **That**: Used to refer to people, animals, or things and is often used in defining relative clauses.
- The dog that barks all night belongs to my neighbor.
- This is the house that Jack built.

6. **Indefinite pronouns** are used to refer to nonspecific persons, places, o things. They don't refer to any particular person or thing, but rather to any one, some, or all of a group.

Here are some examples of indefinite pronouns:

1. **Some**: Can be used as both an indefinite pronoun and a determiner. Examples Somebody called while you were out.
   - Can I have some water, please?
2. **Any**: Used in questions, negatives, and for emphasis.
   Examples: Is there any cake left?
   - I don't have any money.
3. **All**: Refers to the whole quantity or extent of something.
   Examples: All of the students passed the exam.
   - She ate all of the cookies.
4. **None**: Indicates the absence of something or no part of it.
   Examples: None of the apples were ripe.
   - There's none left.
5. **Many**: Refers to a large but indefinite number or quantity.
   Examples: Many people attended the concert.
   - I've visited many countries.
6. **Few**: Refers to a small number or quantity.
   Examples: Few students completed the assignment on time.
   There were few people at the party.
7. **Several**: Refers to more than two but not many.
   Examples: Several books were missing from the shelf.
   We visited several museums during our trip.
8. **Anybody/Anyone**: Refers to any person, no matter who.
   Examples: Does anybody know the answer?
   - Anyone can participate in the contest.
9. **Somebody/Someone**: Refers to a person of unspecified identity. Examples Someone is knocking at the door.
   - Somebody left their jacket here.
10. **Everybody/Everyone**: Refers to all people.
    Examples: Everyone should bring their own lunch.
    Everybody loves a good story.
11. **Nobody/No one**: Refers to no person, not anyone.
    Examples: Nobody knows the answer.
    No one showed up for the meeting.

These indefinite pronouns are handy for referring to unspecified or general quantities, persons, or things in a sentence

7. **Reflexive pronouns** are used when the subject and the object of a sentence are the same person or thing. They end in -self for singular forms and -selves for plural forms. Here are some examples:

1. **Singular Reflexive Pronouns:**
- **Myself**: I hurt myself while cooking.
- **Yourself**: Did you buy the tickets yourself?
- **Himself**: He taught himself how to play the guitar.
- **Herself**: She found herself lost in the unfamiliar city.
- **Itself**: The cat cleaned itself after eating.

2. **Plural Reflexive Pronouns:**
- **Ourselves**: We painted the house ourselves.
- **Yourselves**: You can help yourselves to some snacks.
- **Themselves**: They prepared the presentation themselves.

Reflexive pronouns are used to emphasize that the action of the verb reflects back on the subject, indicating that the subject is performing the action on itself or themselves.

8. **Intensive pronouns,** also known as emphatic pronouns, are pronouns that emphasize or intensify a noun or pronoun in a sentence. They are identical in form to reflexive pronouns but serve a different grammatical function. Here are some examples of intensive pronouns used in sentences:

1. I **myself** completed the project.
- In this sentence, myself emphasizes the subject I, indicating that the speaker completed the project personally.

2. She cooked the entire meal **herself**.
- Here, herself emphasizes the subject She, highlighting that she cooked the entire meal without assistance.

3. He didn't need any help; he fixed the car **himself**.
- Himself emphasizes the subject He, indicating that he fixed the car on his own.

4. The president made the decision **himself**.
- In this sentence, himself emphasizes the noun president, indicating that the president personally made the decision.

5. They built the house **themselves**.
- Themselves emphasizes the subject They, indicating that they built the house without hiring others to do it.

# Adjectives

| | | | |
|---|---|---|---|
| Able | Accepting | Delightful | Bold |
| Brave | Calm | Caring | Cheerful |
| Clever | Complex | Confident | Dependable |
| Dignified | Emphatetic | Energetic | Extroverted |
| Friendly | Giving | Happy | Helpful |
| Idealistic | Independent | Ingenious | Intelligent |
| Introverted | Kind | Knowledgeable | Logical |
| Loving | Mature | Modest | Nervous |
| Observant | Organized | Patient | Powerful |
| Proud | Quiet | Reflective | Relaxed |
| Religious | Responsive | Searching | Self-assertive |
| Self-conscious | Sensible | Sentimental | Shy |
| Silly | Spontaneous | Sympathetic | Tense |
| Trustworthy | Warm | Wise | Witty |

# ADJECTIVES

Adjectives can be used to describe the qualities of noun or pronoun independently or in comparison to something else.
Kinds of adjectives:
1. **Descriptive adjectives** are words that modify or describe nouns or pronouns by providing additional information about their qualities, characteristics, or attributes. They help to give a clearer picture or convey a specific detail about the noun they are referring to. Here are some examples of descriptive adjectives:
1. **Color**: Examples include red, blue, green, yellow, purple, orange, etc.
·Example sentence: She wore a beautiful red dress to the party.
2. **Size**: Examples include big, small, tiny, large, gigantic, minuscule, etc.
·Example sentence: The small kitten played with a big ball of yarn.
3. **Shape**: Examples include round, square, triangular, oval, circular, etc.
·Example sentence: He picked up a round pebble from the beach.
4. **Texture**: Examples include smooth, rough, soft, hard, silky, prickly, etc.
·Example sentence: The soft blanket kept her warm on the chilly night.
5. **Age**: Examples include old, young, ancient, new, modern, antique, etc.
·Example sentence: The old oak tree provided shade on hot summer days.
6. **Origin**: Examples include French, Chinese, American, Italian, British, etc.
·Example sentence: She ordered a delicious Italian pizza for dinner.
7. **Material**: Examples include wooden, metallic, plastic, leather, silk, cotton, etc.
·Example sentence: He bought a sturdy wooden desk for his study.
8. **Condition**: Examples include clean, dirty, broken, new, used, rusty, etc.
·Example sentence: She found a shiny new coin on the sidewalk.
9. **Personality**: Examples include kind, brave, friendly, intelligent, funny, serious, etc.
·Example sentence: He has a kind heart and always helps those in need.

2. **Quantitative adjectives** are words used to describe the quantity or number of nouns in a sentence. They provide information about the amount or quantity of the noun they modify.

Here are some examples of quantitative adjectives:
1. **Many**: There are many apples in the basket.
2. **Few**: There are few opportunities left.
3. **Several**: Several students scored high marks in the exam.
4. **Some**: Can you give me some water?
5. **Any**: Do you have any questions?
6. **All**: All students must attend the assembly.
7. **No**: There are no pens on the table.
8. **Enough**: We have enough food for everyone.
9. **Whole**: The whole town celebrated the victory.
10. **Half**: She ate half of the cake.

3. **Numeral adjectives** are words used to quantify or enumerate nouns. They indicate the number or order of things in a sentence. Here are the main types of numeral adjectives along with examples:

1. **Cardinal Numerals**: These indicate quantity or how many of something there are. One, two, three, four, five, etc.
·Example: There are five apples on the table.
2. **Ordinal Numerals**: These indicate the order of things.
·First, second, third, fourth, fifth, etc.
·Example: He finished in second place in the race.
3. **Multiplicative Numerals**: These indicate the number of times something happens.
·Single, double, triple, quadruple, etc.
·Example: She ordered a double espresso.
4. **Fractional Numerals**: These indicate a part of a whole.
·Half, quarter, third, etc.
·Example: He ate a quarter of the pizza.
5.**Collective Numerals**: These indicate a group or a set.
·Couple, dozen, score, hundred, thousand, etc.
·Example: She bought a dozen roses for her mother.
6. **Distributive Numerals**: These indicate distribution among individuals.
·Each, every, either, neither, etc.
·Example: Each student received a certificate.
7. **Negative Numerals**: These indicate a lack of quantity.
·None, no, zero, etc.
·Example: There are no cookies left in the jar.

**4. Demonstrative adjectives** are words used to indicate or point out specific nouns in a sentence. They help provide clarity by specifying whether the noun is near or far in relation to the speaker. In English, there are four demonstrative adjectives: this, that, these, and those. Here's an explanation with examples:
1.**This**: Used to indicate a singular noun that is close to the speaker.
·Example: This book is interesting. (The book is near the speaker.)
2.**That**: Used to indicate a singular noun that is farther away from the speaker.
·Example: That car is expensive. (The car is farther from the speaker.)
3.**These**: Used to indicate plural nouns that are close to the speaker.
·Example: These cookies are delicious. (The cookies are near the speaker.)
4.**Those**: Used to indicate plural nouns that are farther away from the speaker.
·Example: Those houses are beautiful. (The houses are farther from the speaker.)
These adjectives not only indicate proximity but also help in distinguishing between singular and plural nouns. They are often followed by the noun they modify to specify exactly which noun is being referred to in a conversation or context.


**5. Proper adjectives** are adjectives derived from proper nouns, such as the names of people, places, or organizations. They typically describe characteristics or qualities associated with the proper noun they originate from. Here are some examples:
- **American**: Derived from the proper noun America. Example: American culture.
- **Shakespearean**: Derived from the proper noun Shakespeare. Example: Shakespearean tragedy.
- **Italian**: Derived from the proper noun Italy. Example: Italian cuisine.
- **Victorian**: Derived from the proper noun Victoria. Example: Victorian architecture.
- **Microsoft**: Derived from the proper noun Microsoft. Example: Microsoft software.
- **Olympic**: Derived from the proper noun Olympics. Example: Olympic games.
- **Tesla**: Derived from the proper noun Tesla. Example: Tesla car.
- **Aristotelian**: Derived from the proper noun Aristotle. Example: Aristotelian philosophy.
- **Islamic**: Derived from the proper noun Islam. Example: Islamic art.
- **Japanese**: Derived from the proper noun Japan. Example: Japanese cuisine.

6. **Interrogative adjectives** are a type of adjective used to ask questions about nouns. They are typically used to gather specific information about an unidentified noun. These adjectives are placed before the noun they modify and are used to inquire about which particular thing or things the speaker is referring to.
Here are some examples of interrogative adjectives:
1. **Which**: Used when the speaker is asking about a specific choice or selection among a group of options.
- ·Which book did you choose?
- ·Which route should we take?
2. **What**: Used to inquire about the nature or identity of something.
- ·What color is your car?
- ·What time does the movie start?
3. **Whose**: Indicates possession or ownership, questioning who something belongs to.
- ·Whose jacket is this?
- ·Whose idea was it to go camping?
4.**Whom**: Used when referring to the object of a verb or preposition, especially in formal English.
- ·Whom did you invite to the party?
- ·To whom should I address this letter?

7. **Possessive adjectives** are used to indicate ownership or possession of something. They modify nouns by showing who or what possesses the noun. In English, there are seven possessive adjectives: my, your, his, her, its, our, and their. Here are examples of each:
1.**My**: Used to show possession by the speaker.
- ·This is my car.
2.**Your**: Used to show possession by the person being addressed (singular).
- ·Is this your book?
3.**His:** Used to show possession by a male.
- ·That's his bike.
4.**Her:** Used to show possession by a female.
- ·I met her parents yesterday.
5.**Its**: Used to show possession by an inanimate object or animal.
- ·The cat is cleaning its fur.
6.**Our:** Used to show possession by a group that includes the speaker.
- We are going to our favorite restaurant.
7.**Their:** Used to show possession by a group that does not include the speaker.

8. **Comparative adjectives** are used to compare two or more things, showing the degree of difference between them. They are often formed by adding -er to the end of the adjective for short adjectives, or by using more before the adjective for longer ones. Here are some examples:

1. **Short Adjectives:**
   - ·Fast    Faster: The cheetah is faster than the lion.
   - ·Tall    Taller: John is taller than Jack.
   - ·Strong    Stronger: Steel is stronger than wood.
2. **Long Adjectives:**
   - ·Beautiful    More beautiful: She is more beautiful than her sister.
   - ·Interesting    More interesting: The book is more interesting than the movie.
   - ·Delicious    More delicious: This cake is more delicious than that one.
3. **Irregular Adjectives:**
   - ·Good    Better: Apples are better than oranges.
   - ·Bad    Worse: Getting a cold is worse than getting a headache.
   - ·Far    Farther/Further: The park is farther from here than the library.

Remember, when comparing two things, you use the comparative form of the adjective. If you're comparing more than two things, you typically use more or less before the adjective.

| Types of Adjectives | Definition | Examples |
| --- | --- | --- |
| Descriptive Adjective | Adjectives of Quality or Descriptive Adjectives show the kind of quality of a person or thing.<br><br>Ex. fat, large, small etc. | Mary is a fat girl.<br><br>She is a strong girl. |
| Quantitative Adjective | Adjectives of quantity show how much quantity of a thing is meant.<br><br>Ex. Some, little, whole, half etc. | Get me a cup of tea.<br><br>Give him a glassful of water. |
| Numeral Adjective | Numeral Adjectives show how many persons or things are meant. This adjective represents numeral value.<br><br>Ex. six, few, second, some etc. | He got a new pen.<br><br>That is her first photo. |
| Demonstrative Adjective | Demonstrative Adjectives point out which person or thing is meant.<br><br>Ex: this, that, these | This is Persian a cat.<br><br>These bowls or made of ceramic. |

| Proper Adjectives | Adjectives formed from proper nouns are called Proper Adjectives.<br><br>Ex: American, Indian, Korean etc. | She likes to watch Korean dramas.<br><br>I am an Indian. |
|---|---|---|
| Interrogative Adjectives | Words which are used with s to ask questions, are called Interrogative Adjectives.<br><br>Ex: when, which, whose etc. | Which one is your book?<br><br>Where is my book? |
| Possessive Adjective | Words used to express who owns or possesses something. This is used in front of a noun.<br><br>Ex: my, own, our, her, his etc. | That is my book.<br><br>This is her pen. |
| Comparative adjectives | Comparative adjectives compare one person or thing with another and enable us to say whether a person or thing has more or less of a particular quality.<br><br>Ex: tall, taller, tallest. Much, more, most etc. | Ram is a tall boy.<br><br>Karan is taller than Ram. |

# COMPARATIVE ADJECTIVES
## GRAMMAR RULES

Adjectives up to two syllables can form the comparative by adding -er; three or more syllables can form the comparative by using "more" before the adjective.

- small >>> smaller than
- high >>> higher than
- expensive >>> more expensive than
- dangerous >>> more dangerous than

### One syllable adjectives ending with a vowel + a consonant

- big >>> bigger than
- thin >>> thinner than
- fat >>> fatter than
- sad >>> sadder than

### Two syllable adjectives ending with "-y"

- lazy >>> lazier than
- easy >>> easier than
- happy >>> happier than
- noisy >>> noisier than

### Adjectives with two rules

- clever >>> cleverer/ more clever than
- pretty >>> prettier/ more pretty than
- friendly >>> friendlier/ more friendly than

### Irregular adjectives

- good >>> better
- bad >>> worse
- far >>> farther
- little >>> less

# SUPERLATIVE ADJECTIVES

A superlative adjective is a type of adjective which is used to express the highest degree of comparison.

## Four rules to remember:

### RULE 1 - ONE SYLLABLE ADJECTIVES, ADD -EST TO THE END

A syllable is a voiced part of a word. For example, the word women has two syllables: wo-men. The word sit has only one syllable. The word computer has three syllables.

cold - the coldest    fast - the fastest    tall - the tallest    long - the longest

**For adjectives ending in 'c-v-c' (consonant-vowel-consonant), double the last letter and then add -est.**

big - biggest    thin - thinnest    sad - saddest    hot - hottest

### RULE 2 - IF THE ADJECTIVE ENDS IN -Y, ADD -EST

if the adjective ends in -y, change it to -i and add -est

angry - the angriest    heavy - the heaviest    busy - the busiest    happy - the happiest

### RULE 3 - 'MOST' IS USED FOR LONG ADJECTIVES

If the adjective is a long word that has two or more syllables, add the word most.

beautiful - the most beautiful          careful - the most careful

dangerous - the most dangerous     difficult - the most difficult

### RULE 4 - IRREGULAR FORMS

These are adjectives that do not form the superlative degrees by adding either –est or most.

good - the best          little - the least

bad - the worst          far - the farthest

# Degrees of comparison

Degrees of comparison, also known as degrees of adjectives or adverbs, refer to the different forms that adjectives and adverbs take to indicate the extent or comparison of qualities. There are three degrees of comparison: positive, comparative, and superlative.

1. **Positive Degree:**
· This is the simplest form of an adjective or adverb, without any comparison. It merely describes a quality without comparing it to anything else.
·Example with an adjective:   She is tall.
·Example with an adverb:   He runs quickly.

2. **Comparative Degree:**
· This form is used to compare two things or people. It is formed by adding    -er   to short adjectives (one or two syllables) or by using more   before the adjective or adverb for longer ones.
·Example with an adjective:   She is taller than her sister.
·Example with an adverb:   He runs more quickly than I do.

3. **Superlative Degree:**
· This form is used to compare three or more things or people. It is formed by adding   -est to short adjectives or by using   most before the adjective or adverb for longer ones.
·Example with an adjective:   She is the tallest girl in her class.
·Example with an adverb:     He runs the most quickly of all the athletes.

It's important to note that irregular adjectives and adverbs may have unique forms in the comparative and superlative degrees, and some may use  less  instead of   more for comparison. Additionally, there are some irregular adjectives and adverbs that don't follow a consistent pattern for forming comparatives and superlatives and must be memorized individually.

## Comparative Levels of Adjectives and Adverbs

| Part of Speech | Positive | Comparative | Superlative |
|---|---|---|---|
| Adjective | low | lower | lowest |
| Adjective | big | bigger | biggest |
| Adjective | fat | fatter | fattest |
| Adverb | highly | more highly | most highly |
| Adverb | widely | more widely | most widely |
| Adverb | easily | more easily | most easily |

| Inconsiderate Adjectives and Adverbs | | |
| --- | --- | --- |
| Positive Degree | Comparative Degree | Superlative Degree |
| good | better | best |
| well | better | best |
| bad | worse | worst |
| badly | worse | worst |
| far | farther | farthest |
| far | further | furthest |
| late | later | later or latest |
| little (amount) | less | least |
| many | more | most |
| much | more | most |
| some | more | most |

# VERB

A verb is the action or state of being in a sentence. Verbs can be expressed in different tenses, depending on when the action is being performed.

Examples: Run, walk, jump, talk, sing, speak, eat, drink, cry, skip, pull, push, fetch, give, make, bake, try, bring, teach, study, etc.

## 1. Action Verbs :

Action verbs, also known as dynamic verbs, are words that express actions or activities that a subject can do. They convey a sense of movement, change, or activity within a sentence. Here are some examples of action verbs:

1. **Run**: She runs every morning before work.
2. **Jump**: The athlete jumps over the hurdle effortlessly.
3. **Swim**: We swim in the ocean during the summer.
4. **Eat**: He eats lunch at noon every day.
5. **Write**: She writes poetry in her spare time.
6. **Speak**: He speaks four languages fluently.
7. **Dance**: They dance salsa at the club on weekends.
8. **Laugh**: The children laugh at the clown's antics.
9. **Play**: We play basketball after school.
10. **Sing**: She sings beautifully in the choir.

These verbs all describe actions that someone or something is performing. They add vitality and movement to sentences, helping to paint a vivid picture of what is happening.

## 2. Linking Verbs :

Linking verbs, also known as copular verbs, are verbs that connect the subject of a sentence with a subject complement. Unlike action verbs, which express an action performed by the subject, linking verbs express a state of being or a condition. They do not show action but rather describe or rename the subject.

Here are some examples of linking verbs:

1. **To be (am, is, are, was, were, be, being, been):**
   - ·She is a doctor.
   - ·They were tired.
   - ·He will be a teacher.
2. **To seem:**
   - ·The movie seems interesting.
   - ·She seems happy.
3. **To become:**
   - ·He became a doctor.
   - ·The weather became colder.
4. **To appear:**
   - ·The situation appears dire.
   - ·She appears confident.
5. **To feel** (when expressing a state of being rather than physical sensation):
   - ·She feels excited.
   - ·He feels proud of his achievement.
6. **To look** (when expressing a state or condition):
   - ·You look tired.
   - ·The flowers look beautiful.
7. **To sound:**
   - ·The music sounds melodious.
   - ·Her voice sounds familiar.
8. **To remain:**
   - ·The issue remains unresolved.
   - ·He remained silent.
9. **To taste** (when describing a state rather than the physical act of tasting)
   - ·The food tastes delicious.
   - ·The water tastes salty.

Remember, with linking verbs, the subject complement either renames or describes the subject. For instance, in the sentence She is a doctor, doctor renames she, describing her profession. Similarly, in The food tastes delicious, delicious describes the taste of the food.

# 3. Helping Verbs (Auxiliary Verbs) :

Helping verbs, also known as auxiliary verbs, are verbs that are used alongside the main verb in a sentence to express nuances of meaning, tense, aspect, or mood. They help the main verb by providing additional information about the action or state being described. Here are some examples:

1. **To indicate tense:**
- · She is singing. (Present continuous tense)
- · They have eaten. (Present perfect tense)
- · He will go. (Future tense)

2. **To indicate aspect:**
- · She has been studying. (Present perfect progressive aspect)
- · They had been waiting. (Past perfect progressive aspect)

3. **To express possibility or necessity:**
- · He should study. (Expressing advice or recommendation)
- · You can go. (Expressing possibility)
- · She must leave. (Expressing necessity or obligation)

4. **To form questions:**
- · Are you coming?
- · Has she finished?
- · Will they arrive on time?

5. **To form negatives:**
- · She is not listening.
- · They have not arrived yet.
- · He cannot swim.

In each of these examples, the helping verbs (is, have, will, has, had, been, should, can, must, are, will, have, cannot) assist the main verbs (singing, eaten, go, singing, waiting, studying, leave, coming, finished, arrive, arrived, swim) in conveying different meanings or grammatical structures.

**Forms of "to be"** -
am, is, are, was, were, be, being, been

**Forms of "to have"**
- have, has, had

**Forms of "to do"**
- do, does, did

**Modal verbs**
- can, could, may, might, must, shall, should, will, would

## 4. Modal Verbs :

Modal verbs are a subset of auxiliary verbs used to express modality, which refers to the speaker's attitude or the likelihood of an action or state of being. They indicate necessity, possibility, ability, permission, obligation, or futurity in a sentence.

Here are some common modal verbs in English along with examples:

1. **Can**: Used to express ability or possibility.
· Example: She can speak Spanish fluently.
2. **Could**: Used to express past ability, polite requests, or hypothetical situations.
· Example: I could swim when I was younger.
3. **May**: Used to express permission or possibility.
· Example: You may leave the room now.
4. **Might**: Similar to may, but often implies a lower probability.
· Example: It might rain later.
5. **Must**: Used to express necessity or strong recommendation.
· Example: You must wear a seatbelt in the car.
6. **Should**: Used to express advice, suggestion, or obligation.
· Example: You should apologize for what you said.
7. **Ought to**: Similar to should, with a stronger sense of obligation.
· Example: You ought to finish your homework before going out.
8. **Will**: Used to express future tense, willingness, or inevitability.
· Example: I will call you tomorrow.
9. **Would**: Used to express hypothetical situations, polite requests, or preferences.
· Example: If I were rich, I would travel the world.
10. **Shall**: Often used in formal or legal contexts, or to make suggestions.
· Example: Shall we go for a walk?

These modal verbs can significantly alter the meaning and tone of a sentence, depending on how they are used.

# Have to

Have to is another way to express necessity or obligation in English. Here are some examples of how have to can be used in sentences:

1. **Necessity**:
   - ·I have to wake up early tomorrow for work.
   - ·We have to buy groceries this weekend.
   - ·She has to study for her exam tonight.

2. **Obligation**:
   - ·Students have to attend classes regularly.
   - ·Employees have to submit their reports by Friday.
   - ·Parents have to take care of their children's well-being.

3. **Prohibition (negative form):**
   - ·You have to wear a helmet when riding a bike.
   - ·We have to follow the rules of the road while driving.
   - ·They have to respect the privacy of others.

4. **Certainty:**
   - ·He has to be at the airport by 3 PM; his flight leaves at 4.
   - ·The restaurant has to be good; it's always packed with people.
   - ·She has to have finished her project by now; the deadline was yesterday.

5. **Preference (informal):**
   - ·I have to say, I prefer tea over coffee.
   - ·He has to go for a run every morning to feel awake.
   - ·We have to watch that TV series together; it's so addictive.

Have to is often used in both spoken and written English to express obligations, necessities, or strong recommendations. It's important to note that have to is more commonly used in everyday language, while must can sometimes convey a stronger sense of necessity or formality.

# Must

Must is a modal verb in English that conveys necessity, obligation, or strong recommendation. Here are some examples of how must can be used in sentences:

**1. Necessity:**
- ·You must wear a seatbelt when driving.
- ·I must finish this report before the meeting tomorrow.
- ·We must buy groceries before the stores close.

**2. Obligation:**
- ·Students must complete their assignments on time.
- ·Employees must adhere to the company's dress code.
- ·Citizens must pay their taxes by April 15th.

**3. Strong recommendation:**
- ·You must try the seafood at that restaurant; it's fantastic.
- ·If you're visiting Paris, you must see the Eiffel Tower.
- ·You must read this book; it will change your perspective.

**4. Prohibition (negative form):**
- ·You must not smoke in this area.
- ·Students must not cheat during exams.
- ·Visitors must not feed the animals at the zoo.

**5. Certainty:**
- ·It must be raining outside; I hear thunder.
- ·She's been working on that project all week; it must be nearly finished.
- ·He must have forgotten his keys; he's locked out of the house.

Remember that the use of must can vary based on context and formality, and it's essential to consider the tone and implications of its usage in different situations.

## Can

The modal verb can is used to express ability, possibility, permission, or potentiality in English. Here are some examples of how  can  can be used in different contexts:

1. **Expressing Ability:**
   - ·I can swim.
   - ·She can speak three languages fluently.
   - ·They can solve complex math problems quickly.

2. **Expressing Possibility:**
   - ·It can rain later, so take an umbrella.
   - ·The meeting can be rescheduled if necessary.
   - ·He can be quite unpredictable sometimes.

3. **Expressing Permission:**
   - ·You can borrow my car if you need it.
   - ·Students can leave the classroom when the bell rings.
   - ·Employees can access the company's online training modules
.
4. **Expressing Requests or Offers:**
   - ·Can you pass me the salt, please?
   - ·Can I help you with your bags?
   - ·I can give you a ride home if you'd like.

5. **Expressing Potentiality or Likelihood:**
   - ·If you study hard, you can pass the exam.
   - ·With proper training, he can become a great athlete.
   - ·This new method can revolutionize the industry.

Remember, the usage of  can  can vary depending on the context and tense. It's also important to note that  can  is the present tense form, while  could  is its past tense form and is often used for polite requests or to express past ability or possibility.

# Will

The word "will" is a versatile modal verb in English, commonly used to express future actions, intentions, beliefs, promises, and more. Here are some examples of how "will" can be used in different contexts:

1. **Future actions:**
   - ·I will go to the store tomorrow. (Expressing a future action.)
   - ·She will arrive at 8 p.m. (Predicting a future event.)
   - ·They will start the project next week. (Indicating a planned future action.)
2. **Intentions or willingness:**
   - ·I will help you with your homework. (Expressing a willingness or intention to help.)
   - ·He will try his best to finish the work on time. (Expressing intention or determination.)
3. **Predictions or beliefs:**
   - ·It will probably rain later today. (Expressing a prediction based on current conditions.)
   - ·She will be successful in her career. (Expressing a belief or prediction about someone's future.)
4. **Promises or commitments:**
   - ·I will always love you. (Making a promise or commitment.)
   - ·They will deliver the goods by Friday. (Committing to a specific action or deadline.)
5. **Requests or offers:**
   - ·Will you pass me the salt, please? (Making a polite request.)
   - ·I will pay for dinner tonight. (Offering to pay for something.)
6. **Habitual actions or characteristics:**
   - ·She will always interrupt others when they speak. (Describing a habitual action.)
   - ·He will forget his keys at least once a week. (Describing a characteristic behavior.)
7. **Conditional statements:**
   - ·If it rains, I will bring an umbrella. (Expressing a future action based on a condition.)
   - ·I will call you if I need help. (Future action contingent upon a condition.)

# May

The word may can be used in several ways in English, primarily as a modal verb to indicate possibility, permission, or to express wishes. Here are some examples of how may can be used in different contexts:

1. **Possibility:**
   - ·It may rain tomorrow. (There is a possibility of rain tomorrow.)
   - ·She may be late for the meeting. (There is a possibility that she will be late.)
   - ·The package may arrive today. (There's a chance the package will arrive today.)

2. **Permission:**
   - ·You may leave the room now. (Permission to leave the room.)
   - ·May I borrow your pen, please? (Requesting permission to borrow a pen.)
   - ·Students may not use calculators during the exam. (Stating a rule or restriction.)

3. **Wishes or hopes:**
   - ·May all your dreams come true. (Expressing a wish for someone's dreams to come true.)
   - ·May you have a safe journey. (Wishing someone a safe journey.)

4. **Formal usage:**
   - ·May I introduce myself? (Used in formal introductions.)
   - ·It may be noted that... (Used in formal or academic writing to introduce a point.)

5. **Probability or likelihood:**
   - ·She may well win the competition. (Indicating a high probability of winning.)
   - ·He may not know the answer. (Suggesting a possibility of not knowing.)

6. **Conditional statements:**
   - ·If you study hard, you may pass the exam. (Expressing a possibility in a conditional statement.)
   - Remember, the usage of may can vary depending on the context and formality of the situation.

# Should

The word should is a modal verb that is commonly used to indicate obligation, expectation, advice, or probability in English. Here are some examples of how should can be used in different contexts:

**1. Obligation or duty:**
- ·You should finish your homework before watching TV. (Expressing a recommendation or obligation.)
- ·Employees should arrive at work on time. (Stating an expected behavior or duty.)

**2. Expectation or likelihood:**
- ·The train should arrive at 10 a.m. (Expressing an expected time or event.)
- ·He should know the answer by now. (Expressing an expectation based on circumstances.)

**3. Advice or suggestion:**
- ·You should eat more vegetables for better health. (Offering advice or making a suggestion.)
- ·She should see a doctor if her symptoms persist. (Suggesting a course of action.)

**4. Probability or possibility:**
- ·It should be sunny tomorrow. (Expressing a high probability based on current conditions.)
- ·The package should arrive within a week. (Expressing an expectation of likelihood.)

**5. Polite requests or offers:**
- ·Should I help you with your bags? (Making a polite offer to assist.)
- ·Should we go out for dinner tonight? (Making a polite suggestion or invitation.)

**6. Expressing preference or desire:**
- ·I should like to visit Paris someday. (Expressing a preference or desire.)
- ·She should prefer tea over coffee. (Indicating a preference.)

**7. Formal usage:**
- ·It should be noted that... (Used in formal or academic writing to introduce a point.)
- ·Should you require any further assistance, please do not hesitate to contact us? (Formal expression offering assistance.)

# Shall

The word shall is a modal verb in English that can be used to indicate a future action, obligation, intention, or suggestion, particularly in formal or legal contexts. Here are some examples of how shall can be used in different contexts:

**1. Future actions:**
- ·I shall meet you at the restaurant at 7 p.m. (Expressing a future action.)
- ·We shall discuss the matter further tomorrow. (Referring to a planned future discussion.)

**2. Obligation or requirement:**
- ·Students shall submit their assignments by Friday. (Stating a requirement or obligation.)
- ·The tenant shall maintain the property in good condition. (Describing a contractual obligation.)

**3. Intentions or plans:**
- ·I shall apply for the job vacancy. (Expressing intention or plan.)
- ·She shall visit her grandparents this weekend. (Referring to a planned visit.)

**4. Suggestion or proposal:**
- ·Shall we go for a walk in the park? (Making a suggestion or proposal.)
- ·Shall I book the tickets for the concert? (Asking if action should be taken.)

**5. Formal usage:**
- ·The board of directors shall convene next month. (Formal statement of future action.)
- ·The parties shall negotiate the terms of the contract. (Formal indication of obligation.)

**6. Legal or contractual language:**
- ·The defendant shall appear in court on the specified date. (Legal requirement.)
- ·The contractor shall indemnify the client against any damages. (Contractual obligation.)

**7. Promise or determination:**
- ·I shall do my best to complete the project on time. (Expressing a promise or determination.)
- ·We shall overcome all obstacles together. (Expressing determination or resolve.)

## Ought to

Ought to is a modal verb used to express obligation, duty, or advisability. Here are some examples of how ought to can be used in sentences:

1. **Obligation/Expectation:**
   - ·You ought to finish your homework before watching TV.
   - ·He ought to apologize for what he said.

2. **Advice/Recommendation:**
   - ·You ought to see a doctor if you're feeling unwell.
   - ·They ought to invest in renewable energy for a sustainable future.

3. **Moral Duty:**
   - ·We ought to help those in need.
   - ·They ought to treat others with respect.

4. **Probability/Expected Outcome:**
   - ·If you study regularly, you ought to do well on the exam.
   - ·With proper maintenance, the car ought to last for many years.

5. **Likelihood in the Past:**
   - ·She ought to have arrived by now.
   - ·They ought to have finished the project already.

Overall, ought to implies a sense of moral obligation, advice, or expectation, indicating what is considered the right or appropriate course of action in a given situation.

## Use of Dare and Need

### Use of Dare and Need

### 1. Dare:
**·As a modal verb to express challenge or defiance:**
- How dare you speak to me like that!
- I dare you to jump off the high diving board.

**·As a main verb to express courage:**
- She dared to speak up against injustice.
- He dared to explore the abandoned house.

### 2. Need:
**·As a modal verb to express necessity or obligation:**
- You need to finish your homework before you can go out.
- We need to address this issue immediately.

**·As a main verb to express requirement:**
- I need some time to think about it.
- She needs assistance with her project.

In summary, dare can be used to express challenge, defiance, or courage, while need is used to express necessity or obligation.

### Summary of Key Points:
- Dare can be used both with and without "to." As a main verb, it often conveys courage or defiance. As a modal verb, it is used to show boldness or challenge.
- Need can also be used both ways, but as a modal verb, it usually means something is unnecessary, and as a main verb, it implies necessity or requirement.

Both verbs add a level of nuance and subtlety depending on how they are used in sentences.

# Used to

Used to is a phrase that indicates a past habitual action or state that no longer occurs in the present. It is often used to describe past habits, customs, or situations that were common or regular but have since changed.

Here are some examples:

1. **Past Habitual Actions:**
   - ·I used to play soccer every weekend when I was younger.
   - ·She used to smoke, but she quit last year.
   - ·They used to live in New York before they moved to California.

2. **Past States:**
   - The house used to be painted blue, but now it's green.
   - ·He used to be really shy, but now he's very outgoing.
   - ·We used to be best friends, but we drifted apart over the years.
   - 

3. **Expressions of Preference or Desire:**
   - ·I used to prefer tea over coffee, but now I enjoy both.
   - ·She used to want to be a doctor, but now she's interested in business.

4. **Contrasts with the Present:**
   - ·I used to be a night owl, but now I'm an early riser.
   - ·They used to eat out every night, but now they cook at home more often.

**Note**: Used to is used to describe past situations that are no longer true in the present. It's important to distinguish used to from use to, which is incorrect. The correct form is always used to.

# Could

The word "could" in English is a modal verb used to express various nuances, including ability, possibility, permission, and polite requests. Here are the primary uses of "could":

## 1. Past Ability
- Describes something someone was able to do in the past.
  - Example: When I was younger, I could run a mile in six minutes.

## 2. Possibility
- Expresses that something is possible but not certain.
  - Example: It could rain later, so take an umbrella.

## 3. Polite Requests
- Makes a request sound more polite or less direct.
  - Example: Could you pass me the salt, please?

## 4. Suggestions
- Used to offer ideas or suggestions.
  - Example: We could go to the park this afternoon.

## 5. Conditional Situations (Hypothetical)
- Used in conditional sentences to indicate what might happen in specific circumstances.
  - Example: If I had more time, I could help you with your project.

## 6. Permission
- Gives or asks for permission in a polite or formal way (less common than "can").
  - Example: You could leave early if you finish your work.

## 7. Uncertainty or Doubt
- Expresses doubt or uncertainty about something.
  - Example: He could be at the library, but I'm not sure.

## 8. Implied Criticism
- Suggests that something was possible but not done, implying a sense of reproach.
  - Example: You could have told me you were running late.

# Would

The word "would" is a modal verb in English used to express various meanings such as hypothetical situations, polite requests, habitual actions in the past, and more. Here are the main uses of "would":

## 1. Hypothetical Situations
- Expresses an imagined or unreal situation, often paired with "if" in conditional sentences.
    - Example: If I were rich, I would travel the world.
    - Example: She would help you if she had the time.

## 2. Future in the Past
- Describes an action that was expected to happen in the future from a past perspective.
    - Example: He said he would call me later.
    - Example: I knew they would win the game.

## 3. Polite Requests or Offers
- Used to make a request or offer sound more polite or formal.
    - Example: Would you like some coffee?
    - Example: I would appreciate it if you could help me.

## 4. Repeated Actions in the Past
- Refers to habitual actions in the past (similar to "used to").
    - Example: When I was a child, I would visit my grandparents every weekend.
    - Example: They would always have tea in the garden.

## 5. Preference
- Expresses a preference or choice.
    - Example: I would rather stay home tonight.
    - Example: He would prefer to take the train instead of driving.

## 6. Speculation or Uncertainty
- Makes assumptions or speculations about past actions or events.
    - Example: That would explain why he was late.
    - Example: She would have been upset if she had known.

## 7. Conditional Past (Unreal Past)
- Refers to something that might have happened but didn't, often with "have" + past participle.
    - Example: If I had studied harder, I would have passed the exam.

# Might

The modal verb "might" in English is used to express possibility, permission, suggestions, and uncertainty. Here's a detailed breakdown of its uses:

**1. Possibility**
- "Might" is used to indicate that something is possible but not certain.
  - Example: It might rain later, so take an umbrella.
  - Example: She might be at home, but I'm not sure.

**2. Polite Suggestions**
- Offers polite advice or suggestions, often softer than "should."
  - Example: You might want to check your email for updates.
  - Example: He might consider applying for that job.

**3. Permission (Formal or Tentative)**
- Indicates permission in formal or hypothetical situations.
  - Example: You might leave early if you finish your work.
  - Example: He might borrow the car if he asks politely.

**4. Uncertainty or Doubt**
- Expresses uncertainty about past actions or events, especially in conjunction with "have" + past participle.
  - Example: She might have forgotten about the meeting.
  - Example: They might have taken a different route.

**5. Hypothetical Situations**
- Used in conditional sentences to describe what is possible in hypothetical or unreal scenarios.
  - Example: If I had more time, I might visit the museum.
  - Example: He might have won if he had trained harder.

**6. Expressing Caution or Softened Statements**
- Used to soften a statement, making it less assertive or direct.
  - Example: You might find this book useful.
  - Example: That might not be the best idea.

# Key Notes:

- **"Might" vs. "May":**
- "May" is often seen as more formal and certain than "might."
- Example: It may rain (more certain). / It might rain (less certain).
- In practice, however, they are often interchangeable when expressing possibility.
- "Might" in the Past:
- To refer to past possibilities or uncertainties, use "might have" + past participle.
- Example: She might have missed the bus.


- **Could" vs. "Can":**
- "Can" refers to present or future ability/possibility, while "could" is used for the past or hypothetical situations.
- Example: I can help you tomorrow (present). / I could help you if I had more time (hypothetical).


- **"Would" vs. "Will":**
- "Will" refers to definite actions in the present or future, while "would" is used for hypotheticals, politeness, or past situations.
- Example: I will go if I can (certain). / I would go if I could (hypothetical).


- **"Would" vs. "Will":**
- "Will" refers to definite actions in the present or future, while "would" is used for hypotheticals, politeness, or past situations.
- Example: I will go if I can (certain). / I would go if I could (hypothetical).

# What are Modal Auxiliaries?

They are helper verbs used to express different conditions, such as possibility, ability, permission, or necessity. They are also used before the main verb (in its infinitive form without the word to). For example, instead of "I plan to learn a new language," use a modal verb and write "I will learn a new language."

| | PURPOSE | EXAMPLE |
|---|---|---|
| can | Expresses ability | I can play the guitar. |
| may | Expresses possibility or permission | She may win the contest. You may borrow my book. |
| might | Expresses possibility | It might rain. |
| could | Expresses possibility or permission | He could learn to ski. Could I skate with you? |
| should | Expresses an obligation | I should wash the dishes. |
| would | Expresses a request | Would you get the mail? |
| will | Expresses intended future action or a request | I will read a book next week. Will you water the garden? |
| must | Expresses a necessity | We must arrive on time. |

## 5. Transitive Verbs :

Transitive verbs are action verbs that require a direct object to complete their meaning. In other words, these verbs act upon something or someone, transferring their action to the object. Here are some examples to illustrate:

1. **She ate the apple.**
 · In this sentence, ate is the transitive verb, and apple is the direct object because it receives the action of eating.
2. **He kicked the ball.**
 · Kicked is the transitive verb here, and ball is the direct object because it receives the action of being kicked.
3. **They built a house.**
 · Built is the transitive verb, and house is the direct object because it receives the action of being built.
4. **I love pizza.**
 · In this case, love is the transitive verb, and pizza is the direct object because it receives the action of being loved.
5. **She read the book.**
 · Read is the transitive verb, and book is the direct object because it receives the action of being read.

## 6. Intransitive Verbs :

Intransitive verbs are action words that do not require a direct object to complete their meaning. In simpler terms, they express an action that doesn't transfer to something or someone else. Here are some examples:

1. **Run**: She runs every morning.
· In this sentence, runs is an intransitive verb because it doesn't need an object to make sense. It stands alone to express the action of running.
2. **Laugh**: The children laughed loudly.
· Laughed is the intransitive verb here. It describes an action without needing an object.
3. **Sleep**: He sleeps peacefully.
· In this sentence, sleeps is an intransitive verb because it expresses the action of sleeping without transferring that action to anything else.
4. **Arrive**: The train arrived on time.
· Arrived is the intransitive verb. It describes the action of reaching a destination without requiring an object.
5. **Disappear**: The magician disappeared suddenly.
· Disappeared is an intransitive verb because it doesn't have a direct object. It expresses the action of vanishing.

# 7. Regular Verbs :

Regular verbs are those that follow a predictable pattern when conjugated in different tenses and moods. They maintain the same root form throughout, with the addition of endings or suffixes to indicate tense, aspect, mood, and agreement with the subject.

1. **Base Form**: This is the form of the verb you find in the dictionary.
· Example: talk
2. **Past Tense**: This form indicates an action that occurred in the past.
· Example: talked
3. **Past Participle**: This form is used in perfect tenses or passive voice constructions.

· Example: talked
Examples of regular verbs in English:
1. **Walk**:
- · Base Form: walk
- · Past Tense: walked
- · Past Participle: walked
· Example: She walks to school every day. Yesterday, she walked to school.
2. **Jump**:
- · Base Form: jump
- · Past Tense: jumped
- · Past Participle: jumped
· Example: He jumps over the fence. He jumped over the fence yesterday.
3. **Play:**
- · Base Form: play
- · Past Tense: played
- · Past Participle: played
· Example: They play soccer every weekend. They played soccer last Saturday.
4. **Dance**:
- · Base Form: dance
- · Past Tense: danced
- · Past Participle: danced
· Example: She dances beautifully. She danced at the party last night.
5. **Cook**:
- · Base Form: cook
- · Past Tense: cooked
- · Past Participle: cooked
· Example: He cooks dinner every evening. He cooked dinner for us last night.

## 8. Irregular Verbs :

Irregular verbs in English are those that don't follow the regular pattern of conjugation in certain tenses. Unlike regular verbs, which typically add -ed to form their past tense and past participle forms, irregular verbs have unique forms for these tenses. Here are some examples:

1. **Go**:
   - Present: I go to school every day.
   - Past: Yesterday, I went to the park.
   - Past Participle: I have gone to that restaurant before.
2. **Eat**:
   - ·Present: I eat breakfast every morning.
   - ·Past: Yesterday, I ate sushi for lunch.
   - ·Past Participle: I have eaten at this restaurant many times.
3. **See**:
   - ·Present: I see my friend at the gym often.
   - ·Past: Last week, I saw a movie with my family.
   - ·Past Participle: I have seen that movie before.
4. **Take**:
   - ·Present: I take the bus to work.
   - ·Past: Last month, I took a vacation to Italy.
   - ·Past Participle: I have taken many photos during my trips.
5. **Run**:
   - ·Present: I run in the park every evening.
   - ·Past: Yesterday, I ran five miles.
   - ·Past Participle: I have run a marathon in the past.

## Regular
### add -ed

| | |
|---|---|
| play | → played |
| visit | → visited |
| mix | → mixed |
| talk | → talked |
| finish | → finished |
| walk | → walked |
| create | → created |

## Irregular
### change spelling

| | |
|---|---|
| say | → said |
| found | → find |
| make | → made |
| know | → knew |
| draw | → drew |
| win | → won |
| run | → ran |

# 9. Finite Verbs :

Finite verbs are action words that show tense (past, present, or future) and agree with the subject in number (singular or plural).
They express actions, occurrences, or states of being within a sentence. Here are some examples:

1. He runs every morning. (Present tense)
   - In this sentence, runs is the finite verb. It shows present tense and agrees with the singular subject he.
2. They ate dinner last night. (Past tense)
   - Ate is the finite verb, indicating past tense and agreeing with the plural subject they.
3. She will sing at the concert. (Future tense)
   - ·Will sing is the finite verb, showing future tense and agreeing with the singular subject she.
4. The students are studying for their exams. (Present continuous tense)
   - Are studying is the finite verb, indicating present continuous tense and agreeing with the plural subject students.
5. He has finished his homework. (Present perfect tense)
   - Has finished is the finite verb, representing present perfect tense and agreeing with the singular subject he.

**Imperative Mood**
- Sentence: Close the window.
  - Explanation: "Close" is finite because it is in the imperative mood, with the implied subject "you."

**Interrogative (Question)**
- Sentence: Does she like ice cream?
  - Explanation: "Does" is finite because it is conjugated to match the third-person singular subject "she," while "like" is in its base form.

**Subjunctive Mood**
- Sentence: I wish he were here.
  - Explanation: "were" is finite because it is in the past subjunctive, expressing a hypothetical situation.

## 10. Non-finite Verbs :

Non-finite verbs are verbs that are not limited by a subject or tense. They don't indicate person, number, or tense. There are three types of non-finite verbs: infinitives, gerunds, and participles.

1. **Infinitives**: Infinitives are the base form of a verb preceded by to. They can function as nouns, adjectives, or adverbs.
Examples:
- ·To swim is my favorite activity. (Here, to swim acts as a noun, serving as the subject of the sentence.)
- ·I want to eat some pizza. (Here, to eat is the object of the verb want.)
- ·He is ready to go. (Here, to go modifies the adjective ready, functioning as an adverb.)

2. **Gerunds**: Gerunds are verbs ending in -ing that function as nouns.
Examples:
- ·Swimming is good exercise. (Here, swimming acts as the subject of the sentence.)
- ·I enjoy reading. (Here, reading is the object of the verb enjoy.)
- ·She is fond of dancing. (Here, dancing acts as the object of the preposition of.)

3. **Participles**: Participles are verb forms that can function as adjectives.
Examples:
- ·The falling leaves covered the ground. (Here, falling modifies the noun leaves.)
- ·The broken window needs to be fixed. (Here, broken describes the noun window.)
- ·We saw a man running after the bus. (Here, running describes the noun man.)

# Verb to be

## simple present

| Singular subject pronouns | Plural subject pronouns |
|---|---|
| I | You |
| You | We |
| He | They |
| She | |
| It | |

| Subject pronouns | Long form | Short form |
|---|---|---|
| I | I am | I'm |
| He | He is | He's |
| She | She is | She's |
| It | It is | It's |
| You | You are | You're |
| We | We are | We're |
| They | They are | They're |

I am here for all this very helpful information.

Exactly, "you are here" is the perfect example.

# ADVERB

An adverb is a word that can modify or describe a verb, adjective, another adverb, or entire sentence.
EX: Adverbs can be used to show manner (how something happens), degree (to what extent), place (where), and time (when).

Different types of adverbs

1.**Conjunctive adverbs:** These are words that connect clauses or sentences, providing transitions between ideas or indicating relationships between them. They serve as bridges between independent clauses within a sentence or between separate sentences.

Here are some common conjunctive adverbs along with examples:

1. **However**: Indicates contrast or contradiction.
   - ·She studied hard; however, she failed the exam.
2. **Moreover**: Adds information or emphasis.
   - ·He was not only a talented musician but moreover an excellent painter.
3. **Therefore**: Shows consequence or conclusion.
   - ·She didn't study for the test; therefore, she failed.
4. **Nevertheless**: Indicates contrast or concession.
   - ·He didn't have much experience; nevertheless, he got the job.
5. **Meanwhile**: Shows simultaneous action or time frame.
   - ·She was cooking dinner; meanwhile, he was setting the table.
6. **Furthermore**: Adds additional information or support.
   - ·The study showed positive results; furthermore, it suggested potential applications.
7. **Otherwise**: Indicates consequence or condition.
   - ·Study hard; otherwise, you won't pass the exam.
8. **Consequently**: Shows result or consequence.
   - ·She missed the bus; consequently, she arrived late to work.
9. **Nonetheless**: Indicates contrast or concession.
   - ·The weather was terrible; nonetheless, they decided to go on the hike.
10. **Similarly**: Shows similarity or comparison.
    - ·She enjoys painting; similarly, her sister loves sculpting.

2. **Adverbs of frequency:** These are words that describe how often an action occurs. They help provide more detail about the frequency of an action in a sentence.
Here are some common adverbs of frequency along with examples:

1. **Always**:
·Example: She always arrives early to class.
2. **Usually**:
·Example: I usually eat breakfast before 8 a.m.
3. **Often**:
·Example: They often go for a walk in the evening.
4. **Sometimes**:
·Example: Sometimes, I like to relax and watch movies on weekends.
5. **Rarely**:
·Example: He rarely misses his morning jog.
6. **Occasionally**:
·Example: They occasionally visit their relatives in the countryside.
7. **Seldom**:
·Example: Seldom does she forget her keys at home.
8. **Never**:
·Example: He never drinks coffee in the evening.

3. **Adverbs of manner:** These are words that modify or describe how an action is performed. They provide more information about the verb in terms of how something is done.
Here are some examples:

1. **Quickly**: She ran quickly to catch the bus.
2. **Carefully**: He handled the fragile vase carefully.
3. **Quietly**: The children whispered quietly during the movie.
4. **Loudly**: The band played loudly at the concert.
5. **Efficiently**: The new software program processes data efficiently.
6. **Gracefully**: The ballerina danced gracefully across the stage.
7. **Briskly**: The wind blew briskly through the trees.
8. **Slowly**: The traffic moved slowly in the rain.
9. **Happily**: They sang happily as they walked along the trail.
10. **Nervously**: She tapped her foot nervously while waiting for her interview.

In each example, the adverb of manner adds more detail to how the action is being performed. They answer questions like how?, in what way? , or to what extent? regarding the action described by the verb.

3. **Adverbs of time:** These are words that describe when an action occurs or for how long it occurs. They provide more information about the timing of an action in relation to the present, past, or future.

Here are some examples of adverbs of time with explanations:

1. **Now**: Indicates the present moment.
·Example:   I am writing now.
2. **Yesterday**: Refers to the day before today.
·Example:   We went to the beach yesterday.
3. **Today**: Refers to the current day.
·Example:   I am busy today.
4. **Tomorrow**: Refers to the day after today.
·Example:   We will have a meeting tomorrow.
5. **Soon**: Indicates in the near future.
·Example:   They will arrive soon.
6. **Later**: Indicates a point in the future, not immediately but after some time.
·Example:   I will call you later.
7. **Early**: Refers to a time before expected or usual.
·Example:   She arrived early for the appointment.
8. **Late**: Refers to a time after expected or usual.
·Example:   He came to the party late.
9. **Always**: Refers to all times or on all occasions.
·Example:   She always arrives early for work.
10. **Never**: Refers to not at any time or not on any occasion.
·Example:   He never misses his morning jog.
11. **Daily**: Refers to something occurring every day.
·Example:   He reads the newspaper daily.
12. **Monthly**: Refers to something occurring every month.
·Example:   She pays her bills monthly.
13. **Yearly**: Refers to something occurring every year.
·Example:   They go on vacation yearly.
14. **Occasionally**: Refers to something happening from time to time, but not regularly.
Example:   She visits her grandparents occasionally.

5. **Adverbs of degree:** These also known as degree adverbs or degree modifiers, are words that modify or intensify the meaning of adjectives, verbs, or other adverbs. They indicate the extent, intensity, or degree of the action or quality being described.

Here are some common examples of adverbs of degree along with explanations and examples:

1. **Very**: Used to intensify the meaning of an adjective or adverb. It indicates a high degree of the quality being described.
   - ·She is very happy.
   - ·It's very cold outside.
2. **Extremely**: Similar to very, but with a stronger emphasis on the intensity.
   - ·The movie was extremely boring.
   - ·He was extremely tired after the long journey.
3. **Quite**: Indicates a moderate degree, often used to suggest a considerable amount but not to the fullest extent.
   - ·She is quite intelligent.
   - ·It's quite cold in this room.
4. **Rather**: Similar to quite, indicating a moderate degree, but with a slightly more formal or reserved tone.
   - ·The test was rather difficult.
   - ·He was rather late to the meeting.
5. **Fairly**: Indicates a moderate degree, similar to quite and rather.
   - ·She's fairly tall for her age.
   - ·The price is fairly reasonable.
6. **Somewhat**: Indicates a small or moderate degree, suggesting a partial fulfillment of the quality being described.
   - ·He was somewhat disappointed with the result.
   - ·The situation is somewhat complicated.
7. **Slightly**: Indicates a small degree, suggesting a minor or barely noticeable amount.
   - ·She's slightly taller than her sister.
   - ·He was slightly amused by the joke.
8. **Enough**: Indicates sufficiency or adequacy.
   - ·She's old enough to make her own decisions.
   - ·He earned enough money to buy the car.

6. **Adverbs of place:** These as the name suggests, provide information about the location or position of an action. They answer the question where? Here are some examples:

1. **Here**: Indicates a location close to the speaker.
·Example:   The keys are here on the table.
2. **There**: Refers to a location away from the speaker but within sight or mentioned earlier in the conversation.
·Example:   She left her bag over there by the door.
3. **Everywhere**: Denotes a location that covers all areas.
·Example:   The children spread their toys everywhere in the room.
4. **Anywhere**: Refers to any unspecified location.
·Example:   You can sit anywhere you like in the classroom.
5. **Somewhere**: Points to an unspecified or unknown location.
·Example:   I think I left my book somewhere in the library.
6. **Upstairs/Downstairs**: Indicates a location relative to a building's floors.
·Example:   She's upstairs in her room studying.
7. **Outside/Inside**: Specifies a location with respect to a boundary or enclosure.
·Example:   It's too noisy outside; let's go inside.
8. **Near/Far**: Provides information about proximity.
·Example:   The grocery store is near our house.

7. **Adverbs of reason:** These as the name suggests, provide information about the reason or cause behind an action or situation. They help answer the question   why?   Here are some examples:

1. **Therefore**: He studied hard; therefore, he passed the exam.
2. **Consequently**: She missed the train; consequently, she arrived late to the meeting.
3. **Accordingly**: The weather was bad; accordingly, the event was canceled.
4. **Hence**: The roads were blocked; hence, we had to find an alternate route.
5. **Thus**: She didn't eat much; thus, she was hungry later.
6. **So**: The restaurant was crowded; so, we decided to eat elsewhere.
7. **Because**: He was tired because he stayed up late studying.
8. **Since**: Since it was raining, we decided to stay indoors.
9. **As a result**: He didn't prepare for the presentation, and as a result, it didn't go well.
10. **For this reason**: She couldn't attend the party; for this reason, she sent her apologies.

| Types | Definition | Examples |
|---|---|---|
| Conjunctive adverbs | Conjunctive adverbs are transition words or phrases. Conjunctive adverbs are also called connective adverbs or linking adverbs. | accordingly, furthermore, moreover, similarly, also, hence, namely, still, anyway, however, nevertheless, then, besides, incidentally, next, |
| Adverbs of frequency | Adverbs of frequency always describe how often something occurs, either in definite or indefinite terms | Often, seldom, rarely, every now and then, hardly ever, sometimes, never, always, occasionally, eventually, etc. |
| Adverbs of time | An adverb of time is a word that describes or modifies when an action occurs. It provides information about the timing or frequency of an action. | Soon now, later, then, tomorrow, today, day after, tomorrow, every day, weekly, annually, quarterly, yearly, yesterday, last |
| Adverbs of manner | An adverb of manner as an adverb that shows how someone does something or how something happens. | badly, loudly, greedily, impatiently, excitedly, quickly, and matter-of-factly. |
| Adverbs of degree | Adverbs of degree tell us about the intensity of something. | almost, barely, entirely, highly, quite, slightly, totally, and utterly |
| Adverbs of place | An adverb of place always describes about the location where the action of the verb is being done. | Up, down, around, away, north, southeast. |
| Adverb of Reason | An adverb of reason provides an explanation for the cause or motivation behind an action. | therefore, thus, consequently, hence, so, accordingly, because, and since. |

# PREPOSITIONS

**Prepositions** are words that show relationships between nouns or pronouns and other words in a sentence. They help us understand the position, location, direction, or timing of things.

## Examples:

- **Position:** "The cat is **on** the table."
- **Location:** "The book is **in** the bag."
- **Direction:** "She walked **towards** the park."
- **Timing:** "We will have lunch **after** the movie."
- **Relationships:** "He is **interested in** science."

Prepositions can also be part of **prepositional phrases**, where they are joined with other words to give more information. For example, '**under the bridge**' or '**on top of the hill**'.

# PREPOSITIONS

A preposition is a word or group of words used before a noun, pronoun, or noun phrase to show direction, time, place, location, spatial relationships, or to introduce an object.

·**Simple** prepositions: location, direction, association
·**Compound** prepositions: above, across, below, between, beneath, within, without etc.
·**Participle** prepositions: considering, during, concerning, provided, following, including, excluding, assuming, regarding, frustrated, given, etc.

**Types of prepositions:**

1.**Prepositions of Place:** These prepositions indicate a location or position. Examples include in, on, at, under, above, below, etc. Here are some examples of prepositions of place:
- **In**: inside or within an enclosed space
    - The cat is sleeping in the box.
    - She lives in New York.
- **On**: above or in contact with a surface
    - The book is on the table.
    - There's a stain on my shirt.
- **At**: near or by a specific point or location
    - Meet me at the corner of the street.
    - We'll be waiting for you at the airport.
- **Under**: below or beneath something
    - The keys are under the mat.
    - The cat is hiding under the bed.
- **Above**: higher than or on top of something
    - The picture is above the fireplace.
    - The plane is flying above the clouds.
- **Below**: lower than or beneath something
    - The temperature is below freezing.
    - The treasure is buried below the ground.
- **Between**: in the space separating two objects or locations
    - The book is between the two bookends.
    - They sat between Mary and John.
- **Among**: surrounded by or in the midst of multiple objects or people
    - The toy is among the other toys in the box.
    - He felt comfortable among his friends.
- **Behind**: at the back or rear of something
    - The car is parked behind the house.
    - The teacher stood behind the students.

# PREPOSITIONS OF PLACE

Prepositions of place tell the position of one thing to another. In the examples below, the prepositions tell where the apple is in relation to the box.

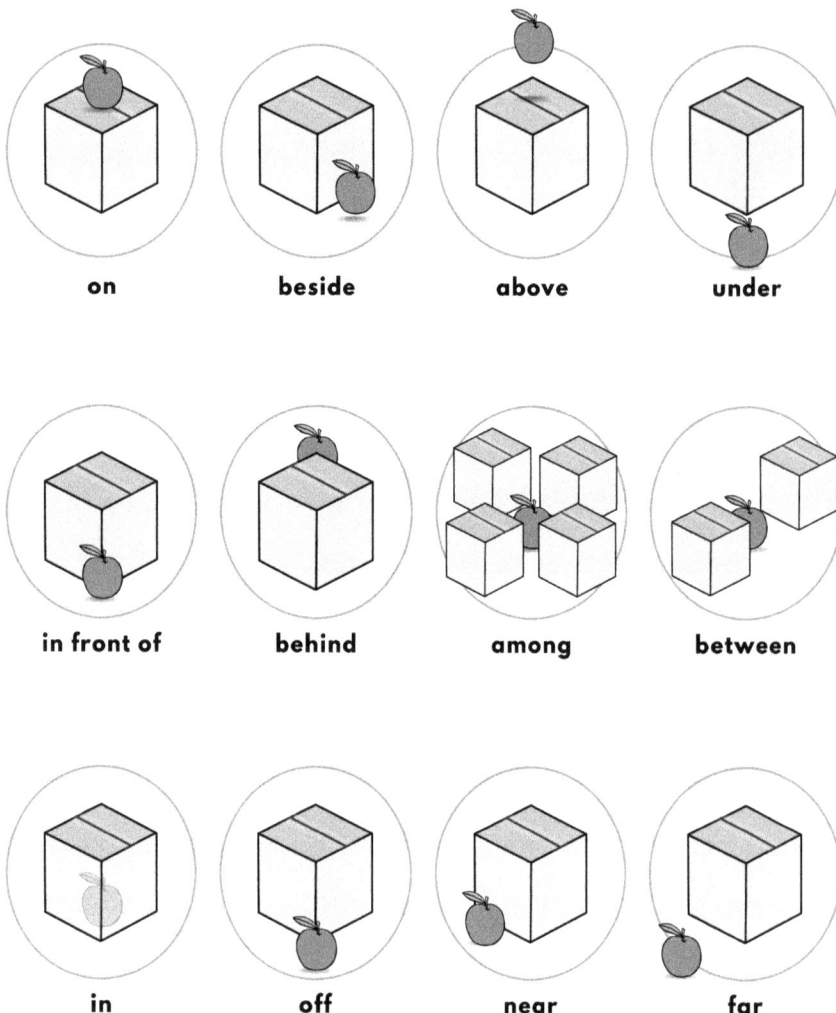

**2. Prepositions of Time:** These prepositions indicate when something happens. Examples include before, after, during, since, until, etc.
Here are some examples of prepositions of time:

1. **At**: used to specify a particular point in time
   - · I have a meeting at 9:00 AM.
   - · They arrived at the party at midnight.

2. **On**: used to specify days and dates
   - · The concert is on Friday.
   - · Our anniversary is on May 15th.

3. **In**: used to indicate longer periods of time, months, years, seasons, or parts of the day
   - · She will graduate in June.
   - · It's too hot to go outside in the summer.
   - · He likes to read in the evening.

4. **Since**: used to indicate the starting point of a period of time or an action that began in the past and continues to the present
   - · I have been working here since 2010.
   - · They have been friends since childhood.

5. **For**: used to indicate the duration of time
   - · She studied for two hours.
   - · They lived in London for five years.

6. **During**: used to indicate when something happens over a period of time
   - · We went for a walk during the afternoon.
   - · He fell asleep during the movie.

7. **Until/ till**: used to indicate the point in time up to which an action or state continues
   · The store is open until 9:00 PM.
   · She waited for her friend until midnight.

8. **Before**: used to indicate the point in time earlier than a specified time
   - · Please arrive before 6:00 PM.
   - · He had never visited Paris before last summer.

3. **Prepositions of Movement or Direction:** These prepositions indicate movement from one place to another. Examples include to, into, onto, through, across, etc.

Here are some examples:

1. **To**: used to indicate movement towards a specific destination
   - · We are going to the beach.
   - · She walked to the store.
2. **From**: used to indicate movement away or starting point
   - · He drove from New York to Boston.
   - · She comes from France.
3. **Toward**(s): used to indicate movement in the direction of something
   - · The dog ran towards the ball.
   - · They are walking towards the park.
4. **Into**: used to indicate movement inside or towards the interior of something
   - · He jumped into the pool.
   - · She went into the house.
5. **Onto**: used to indicate movement onto a surface or platform
   - · The cat jumped onto the table.
   - · They climbed onto the roof.
6. **Out of**: used to indicate movement from the interior or surface of something to the exterior
   - · She stepped out of the car.
   - · The bird flew out of the cage.
7. **Up**: used to indicate movement in a higher position or direction
   - · They walked up the stairs.
   - · The balloon floated up into the sky.
8. **Down**: used to indicate movement in a lower position or direction
   - · He climbed down the ladder.
   - · She slid down the hill.
9. **Across**: used to indicate movement from one side to another, often horizontally
   - · They walked across the bridge.
   - · She swam across the river.
10. **Along**: used to indicate movement in a continuous line or direction
    - · They walked along the beach.
    - · He drove along the highway.

4. **Prepositions of Agent or Instrument:** Prepositions of agent or instrument indicate the means or agent by which an action is performed. They typically show the relationship between the subject of a sentence and the tool or agent used to carry out the action. Some common prepositions used for this purpose include by, with, and via. Here are explanations and examples of each:

- **By**: This preposition is commonly used to indicate the agent performing an action.

Example: The book was written by John.

In this sentence, by shows that John is the one who wrote the book.

- **With**: This preposition is used to indicate the instrument or means used to perform an action.

Example: She cut the cake with a knife.

Here, with shows that the knife is the tool used to cut the cake.

- **Via**: This preposition indicates the route or medium by which something is transmitted or communicated.

Example: The message was sent via email.

Via in this sentence indicates that email was the medium through which the message was sent.

5. **Prepositions of Purpose or Reason**: Prepositions of purpose or reason are used to indicate why something is done or to specify the intention behind an action. They help clarify the purpose or reason for an action or event. Here are some common prepositions used for this purpose, along with examples:

- **For**: For is used to indicate the purpose or reason for an action.

·Example: She went to the gym for exercise.

- **To**: To can also denote purpose or reason, especially when it precedes an infinitive verb.

·Example: He studied hard to pass the exam.

- **In order to**: This phrase is used to express purpose more explicitly.

·Example: She woke up early in order to catch the first train.

- **So as to**: Similar to in order to, it expresses purpose or reason.

·Example: He whispered quietly so as not to wake the baby.

- **With the aim of**: This phrase indicates the intended purpose or goal of an action.

·Example: They organized the event with the aim of raising funds for charity.

# PREPOSITIONS

They show relationships between other words in a sentence, according to the following categories.

## LOCATION

above
after
below
behind
beneath
between
by
in
in front of
into
next to
on
over
under

## MOVEMENT

across
around
against
away
from
into
from
on
onto
off
over
past
to
through
towards
up

## TIME

at
ago
before
in
on
during
for
until
till
since

## A preposition always needs an object.

The object of the preposition is a noun (or word/phrase acting as a noun) that follows a preposition and completes its meaning.

Aika drove her truck to the beach.

object of the preposition → the beach
preposition → to

## A prepositional phrase has three parts.

It has the preposition, the object of the preposition, and the modifiers of the object.

The clownfish swam away from the gigantic shark.

Prepositional phrase → away from the gigantic shark
preposition → from
modifier → gigantic
object → shark

118

# CONJUNCTIONS

**Conjunctions** are special words that connect different parts of a sentence, phrases, or words together. They act like bridges, helping to join ideas, actions, or thoughts.

Types

1.**Coordinating Conjunctions**: Coordinating conjunctions are words used to connect words, phrases, or clauses that are grammatically equal in a sentence. They join elements that are of the same type or importance. There are seven coordinating conjunctions in English:

1.**For**: Used to explain the reason or purpose.
·Example: She went to the store, for she needed some groceries.
2.**And**: Connects words, phrases, or clauses that are similar or related.
·Example: He likes to read books and play video games.
3.**Nor**: Used in negative sentences to connect alternatives.
·Example: She neither sings nor dances.
4.**But**: Shows contrast or exception.
·Example: He wants to go out, but it's raining heavily.
5.**Or**: Presents alternatives or choices.
·Example: Would you like tea or coffee?
6.**Yet**: Shows contrast or unexpected result.
·Example: She studied hard, yet she failed the exam.
7.**So**: Indicates result, consequence, or inference.
·Example: It started raining, so we decided to stay indoors.
These conjunctions are called coordinating because they join elements of equal grammatical rank. They link independent clauses, phrases, or words within a sentence without subordinating one to the other.

2. **Subordinating Conjunctions**: Subordinating conjunctions are words that join independent clauses (complete sentences) with dependent clauses (incomplete thoughts). They indicate a relationship between the two clauses, showing how one idea depends on or is related to the other.

Here are some common subordinating conjunctions along with examples:

1. **Because**: It indicates a cause-and-effect relationship.
· Example: She went to bed early because she was tired.
2. **Although/Though**: These indicate contrast or concession.
· Example: Although it was raining, they went for a walk.
3. **If**: It introduces a condition.
· Example: If you study hard, you will pass the exam.
4. **While**: It indicates a simultaneous action or contrast.
· Example: She sang while she cooked dinner.
5. **Before**: It denotes time relationships.
· Example: Finish your homework before you watch TV.
6. **Since**: It can denote time or cause.
· Example: Since it was raining heavily, they decided to stay indoors.
7. **After**: It denotes a time relationship, indicating that something happens subsequent to another event.
· Example: After she finished her work, she went for a walk.
8. **Unless**: It introduces a condition where something will only happen if a particular condition is not met.
· Example: He won't pass the test unless he studies.
9. **Whenever**: It indicates any time that something happens.
· Example: Whenever it rains, I stay indoors.
10. **Whereas**: It shows a sharp contrast or contradiction.
· Example: She likes coffee, whereas he prefers tea.

These are just a few examples, but there are many other subordinating conjunctions in English. They are essential for creating complex sentences with varied structures and conveying a wide range of meanings.

3. **Correlative Conjunctions**: Correlative conjunctions are pairs of conjunctions that work together to join words, phrases, or clauses of equal importance within a sentence. They often come in pairs, connecting similar grammatical elements. Here are some common correlative conjunctions:

1. **Both...and:** It connects two elements, indicating that both are true or applicable.
· Example: Both Jane and John enjoy hiking.

2. **Either...or**: It presents a choice between two options.
· Example: You can either come to the party tonight or stay home and relax.

3. **Neither...nor**: It indicates that both elements are not true or applicable.
· Example: Neither Sarah nor Tom has finished their homework.

4. **Not only...but also**: It emphasizes additional information.
· Example: She is not only intelligent but also hardworking.

5. **Whether...or**: It presents a choice between alternatives.
· Example: Whether you like it or not, we have to leave now.

6. **As...as**: It indicates equality or comparison.
· Example: He is as tall as his brother.

7. **Such...that**: It expresses a result or consequence.
· Example: It was such a hot day that we decided to stay indoors.
Correlative conjunctions help create balance and clarity in sentences by linking related ideas or choices.

Each type of conjunction serves a specific purpose in connecting elements within a sentence or between sentences.

# CONJUNCTIONS

Conjunctions join together two ideas.

**F**or — gives a reason why

**A**nd — joins similar ideas

**N**or — negative form of "or"

**B**ut — shows a contrast

**O**r — gives a choice

**Y**et — give a contrast

**S**o — shows cause and effect

# INTERJECTIONS

**Interjections** are words that stand alone and often come at the beginning or sometimes in the middle of a sentence. They can show excitement, surprise, joy, frustration, or other strong emotions.

## Examples:

- **Surprise:** "**Wow!** That magic trick was amazing!"
- **Excitement:** "**Yay!** It's finally the weekend!"
- **Agreement:** "**Yes,** I agree with you completely."
- **Frustration:** "**Ugh,** I can't believe I forgot my bag!"
- **Greeting:** "**Hello,** everyone! Good morning!"

Interjections can include words like 'wow,' 'oh,' 'yay,' 'ouch,' 'oops,' 'hey,' 'bravo,' 'alas,' and many more!

# INTERJECTIONS

An interjection is a part of speech that expresses emotions, feelings, or reactions. There are several types of interjections, including:

**1. Expressing Strong Emotion**
- Joy: "I finally got the job!"
- Anger: "Stop that right now!"
- Surprise: "You scared me!"

**2. Giving a Command or Directive**
- Urgent command: "Watch out for the car!"
- Instructional command: "Stand up straight!"

**3. Showing Enthusiasm or Excitement**
- "Congratulations on your graduation!"
- "Happy Birthday!"

**4. Expressing Urgency or Alarm**
- "Fire! Everyone evacuate!"
- "Help! Someone call 911!"

**5. Emphasizing Strong Agreement or Disagreement**
- Agreement: "Yes! That's exactly what I mean!"
- Disagreement: "No! That's not true!"

**6. Expressing Sarcasm or Humor (Often in Casual Writing)**
- "Oh, great! Another meeting!" (sarcastic)
- "Wow, that went well!" (humorously)

Interjections are words or phrases that express strong emotion or reaction. Here's a list of common interjections, along with examples in sentences:

1. **Wow** – expresses amazement or surprise
    - "Wow! That performance was incredible!"
2. **Oh** – shows realization, surprise, or disappointment
    - "Oh, I didn't realize you were here already."
3. **Ouch** – expresses pain
    - "Ouch! I stubbed my toe on the table."
4. **Yay** – shows happiness or excitement
    - "Yay! We finally won the game!".

5. **Oops** – indicates a mistake
   - "Oops! I dropped my phone again."

6. **Hey** – used to call attention or greet
   - "Hey! Are you coming to the party later?"

7. **Ugh** – shows frustration or disgust
   - "Ugh, I can't believe it's raining again!"

8. **Bravo** – expresses praise or approval
   - "Bravo! You did an amazing job with that speech."

9. **Hooray** – celebrates success or joy
   - "Hooray! We finished the project ahead of schedule."

10. **Phew** – indicates relief
    - "Phew, I almost missed my flight!"

11. **Aha** – shows a sudden realization
    - "Aha! I finally understand how to solve this puzzle."

12. **Ew** – expresses disgust
    - "Ew, this milk tastes sour!"

13. **Yikes** – conveys alarm or concern
    - "Yikes! That car came out of nowhere!"

14. **Alas** – expresses sorrow or regret
    - "Alas, we didn't make it in time."

Each interjection helps convey an immediate emotional reaction, adding expressiveness to everyday language.

# FIGURES OF SPEECH

**Figurative language involves using words or expressions beyond their literal meanings to create a specific effect.**

## Simile

A simile is the comparison of two things using like or as.

Example: The girl's nose was as red as a beet.

## Metaphor

A metaphor is a comparison between two unlike things.

Example: She's drowning in a sea of grief.

## Hyperbole

Hyperbole is a great exaggeration not meant to be taken literally.

Example: The girl exploded with anger.

## Alliteration

Alliteration is the repetition of consonants at the beginning of closely connected words.

Example: The boy's skin sizzled in the sun.

## Onomatopoeia

Onomatopoeia is the use of words that sound like the thing they describe.

Example: As the young boy ate his cereal, it snapped, crackled, and popped.

## Personification

Personification is when an inanimate object is given human characteristics.

Example: The sun smiled down on her.

# Figures of Speech

Figures of speech are linguistic devices used to enhance or emphasize the meaning, beauty, or impact of language. Some common figures of speech include:

1. **Simile**: a simile is a figure of speech that directly compares two different things using the words like or as to highlight a similarity between them. It's a way to make descriptions more vivid and engaging. Here's how it works:

1. **Using like** : When using like in a simile, you're directly stating that one thing resembles another in some way.
·Example: Her smile was like sunshine on a rainy day.
·In this example, the simile compares her smile to sunshine, suggesting that her smile brings warmth and brightness just like sunshine does.

2. **Using as** : When using as in a simile, you're making a direct comparison between two things, often highlighting a particular quality or characteristic.
·Example: He fought like a lion defending its territory.
·Here, the simile compares his fighting style to that of a lion, emphasizing his bravery and ferocity.

Similes are effective tools in writing because they create vivid imagery and help readers better understand and visualize the subject being described. They add depth and emotion to language, making it more expressive and engaging.

- As brave as a lion – Comparing someone's bravery to that of a lion.
- He ran like the wind – Suggesting someone ran very fast, like the wind.
- Her smile was as bright as the sun – Comparing a smile's brightness to the sun.
- The water sparkled like diamonds – Comparing the sparkle of water to the shine of diamonds.
- As quiet as a mouse – Indicating someone or something is very quiet.

*Definition*: A comparison between two things using the words "like" or "as."
*Example*: "Her smile was as bright as the sun."
This simile compares a smile to the brightness of the sun, emphasizing its warmth and radiance.

2. **Metaphor**: a metaphor is a figure of speech that directly refers to one thing by mentioning another. It asserts that one thing is another thing, not just that it's like another thing. Metaphors are often used to add richness, depth, and imagery to language. Here are some examples:

1. **Life is a journey.**
· In this metaphor, life is not literally a journey, but the comparison suggests that life involves traveling through various experiences and stages, encountering different obstacles and destinations.

2. **Her voice is music to my ears.**
· This metaphor compares the sound of her voice to the pleasant and harmonious qualities of music, implying that it brings joy and comfort.

3. **The world is a stage.**
· This metaphor, famously coined by William Shakespeare, suggests that life is like a theatrical performance, with individuals playing different roles and engaging in various acts and scenes.

4. **He has a heart of stone.**
· This metaphor characterizes someone as lacking empathy or emotion, likening their heart to an inanimate object, stone, which is typically associated with hardness and coldness..

- Time is a thief – Suggesting time stealthily takes away moments from life.
- Her voice is music to my ears – Comparing her voice to something melodious and pleasing.
- The world is a stage – Implying life is like a performance, and everyone has a role to play.
- He has a heart of stone – Suggesting someone is emotionally unyielding or cold.
- The classroom was a zoo – Describing the classroom as chaotic and noisy.

*Definition:* A direct comparison between two unrelated things, saying one is the other.
*Example:* "Time is a thief."
This metaphor implies that time takes things from us (like memories or youth) without directly stating it.

3. **Personification**: Personification is a literary device where human qualities or attributes are given to non-human entities, objects, or concepts. It's a way of making these non-human things seem more vivid, relatable, or alive. In grammar, personification is often used to add depth or imagery to writing. Here are some examples:

1. **The wind whispered through the trees.**
·In this example, the wind is given the human quality of whispering, which is something humans do, even though the wind itself can't literally speak.

2. **The stars danced in the night sky.**
·Here, stars are personified by being described as dancing, which is a human activity.

3. **The sun smiled down on the children playing in the park.**
·The sun is personified by being described as smiling, a human expression.

4. **The flowers nodded their heads in agreement.**
·Flowers are given the human action of nodding, which is typically associated with understanding or agreement.

5. **The river sang a soothing melody as it flowed past the old mill.**
·The river is personified by being described as singing, an activity associated with humans.

- The wind whispered through the trees – Suggesting the wind can whisper like a person.
- The sun smiled down on us – Attributing the sun with the human act of smiling.
- The car groaned as it climbed the hill – Giving the car a human-like reaction of groaning.
- The flowers danced in the breeze – Describing flowers as if they can dance.
- Time marches on – Treating time as if it actively moves forward like a person.

*Definition:* Giving human qualities or actions to non-human things.
*Example:* "The wind whispered through the trees."
Here, the wind is given the human action of whispering, suggesting a gentle, quiet movement.

## 4. Hyperbole

**Hyperbole**: Hyperbole is a figure of speech in which exaggeration is used for emphasis or effect. In grammar, hyperbole is often used to make a point more forcefully or to create a vivid image in the reader's or listener's mind. Here are some examples:

1. I'm so hungry I could eat a horse.
· This statement exaggerates hunger to emphasize just how hungry the person is.

2. She's as light as a feather.
· This phrase exaggerates someone's weightlessness to emphasize how light she feels.

3. I've told you a million times to clean your room!
· This statement exaggerates the number of times the speaker has asked, emphasizing frustration or impatience.

4. He's the slowest runner in the world.
· This statement exaggerates the person's lack of speed to emphasize how slow he is compared to others.

5. She's got a smile that stretches from ear to ear.
· This phrase exaggerates the width of someone's smile to emphasize its size and brightness.

6. I'm so tired, I could sleep for a week.
· This statement exaggerates exhaustion to emphasize just how tired the person feels.

- I've told you a million times to clean your room – An exaggerated way of saying it's been said many times.
- I'm so hungry I could eat a horse – Expressing extreme hunger with a humorous exaggeration.
- She cried a river of tears – Overstating how much someone cried.
- This bag weighs a ton – Exaggerating the heaviness of the bag.
- I had to wait forever for the bus – Overemphasizing a long wait.

*Definition:* An exaggerated statement used for emphasis or humor.

*Example:* "I'm so hungry I could eat a horse."

This is an exaggeration meant to show extreme hunger.

5. **Alliteration**: Alliteration is a literary device that involves the repetition of consonant sounds at the beginning of nearby or closely connected words. It's often used in poetry, prose, slogans, and even in everyday language to create rhythm, emphasize certain words or ideas, or make phrases more memorable.

Here are some examples:

1. **Peter Piper picked a peck of pickled peppers.**
· In this famous tongue twister, the repetition of the p sound at the beginning of each word creates a rhythmic and memorable phrase.

2. **Sally sells seashells by the seashore.**
· Again, the repetition of the s sound creates a musical quality to the phrase.

3. **She sells sea shells on the sea shore.**
· Another example with the repetition of the s sound.

4. **Garry's giraffe gobbled gooseberries greedily.**
· Here, the repetition of the g sound emphasizes the actions of the giraffe and makes the sentence more vivid.

5. **Crisp crusts crackled and crunched.**
· In this example, the repetition of the cr sound mimics the sound of something being eaten or broken.

- **Peter Piper picked a peck of pickled peppers** – A classic tongue twister with repeated P sounds.
- **She sells seashells by the seashore** – Another tongue twister with repeated S sounds.
- **The wild winds whistled through the willows** – Repetition of the W sound.
- **Busy bees buzzed by the blooming blossoms** – Repeated B sounds.
- **Tim's tiny turtle took a tumble** – Repetition of the T sound.

*Definition:* The repetition of the same initial consonant sound in closely connected words.

*Example:* "Peter Piper picked a peck of pickled peppers." The repeated "p" sound creates a musical rhythm and makes the phrase memorable.

6. **Onomatopoeia**: Onomatopoeia is a figure of speech in grammar where a word imitates the sound it represents. Essentially, it's when a word sounds like the noise it is describing. This literary device is often used to add vividness and sensory detail to writing, making descriptions more lively and engaging.

Here are some examples of onomatopoeic words:

1. **Buzz** – The sound made by bees or a vibrating phone.'
2. **Crash** – The noise of something breaking or colliding.
3. **Hiss** – The sound of a snake or escaping steam.
4. **Bang** – A loud, explosive sound, like a gunshot or door slamming.
5. **Moo** – The sound made by a cow.
6. **Splash** – The sound of something hitting water.
7. **Boom** – A loud, deep, resonating sound, like thunder or an explosion.
8. **Whisper** – The soft sound of someone speaking quietly.
9. **Clap** – The sound of hands striking together.
10. **Sizzle** – The sound of something frying in a pan.

Onomatopoeia brings sounds to life in writing, creating a vivid sensory experience for the reader.

*Definition:* Words that imitate the sounds they describe.
*Example:* "The bees buzzed around the garden."
The word buzzed mimics the actual sound that bees make.

7. **Oxymoron**: An oxymoron is a figure of speech that combines contradictory terms or ideas to create a unique effect, often to emphasize a point or create a vivid image. In grammar, oxymoron is formed by placing two contradictory words or phrases next to each other, creating a sort of linguistic tension.

Here are some examples:

1.**Jumbo shrimp**:
  The word jumbo typically implies something large, while shrimp suggests something small. When combined, they create an oxymoron, highlighting the contradiction between size and delicacy.

2.**Deafening silence:**
Deafening means extremely loud, while silence implies the absence of sound. This oxymoron emphasizes the profound quietness by describing it with a term usually associated with noise.

3.**Living dead**:
Living suggests vitality and activity, while  dead implies the absence of life. This phrase is commonly used to describe zombies or situations where people seem to be alive but lack vitality.

4.**Bittersweet**:
Bitter  refers to something unpleasant or harsh, while   sweet denotes something pleasant or enjoyable. This oxymoron captures the complexity of emotions, where something can be simultaneously both painful and pleasurable.

8. **Irony**: A contrast between expectation and reality.

This happens when there is a discrepancy between what is expected to happen and what actually occurs.
- Example: A fire station burns down.
- Context: One would expect a fire station to be the least likely place for a fire to happen.

Definition: A contrast between expectation and reality, often highlighting the opposite of what is intended.

Example: "A fire station burned down."

This is ironic because one would expect a fire station, of all places, to be safe from fire.

# THE TENSE

The tense refers to the time at which an action or state of being takes place. There are three primary tenses in English: past, present, and future. Each tense can also be further divided into simple, continuous (progressive), perfect, and perfect continuous forms, allowing for precise expression of when an action occurs relative to the present, past, or future.

| TENSES | TENSES FORMS |
|---|---|
| Present Tense | 1. Simple Present Tense<br>2. Present Perfect Tense<br>3. Present Continuous Tense<br>4. Present Perfect Continuous Tense |
| Past Tense | 1. Simple Past Tense<br>2. Past Perfect Tense<br>3. Past Continuous Tense<br>4. Past Perfect Continuous Tense |
| Future Tense | 1. Simple Future Tense<br>2. Future Perfect Tense<br>3. Future Continuous Tense<br>4. Future Perfect Continuous Tense |

| Tenses | Rules and Formula | Examples |
|---|---|---|
| Simple Present Tense | Subject + Verb in the base form/third person plural form + the rest of the sentence | <ul><li>She walks to school every day.</li><li>He plays basketball with his friends on weekends.</li><li>The sun rises in the east.</li><li>They speak French fluently.</li></ul> |
| Present Continuous Tense | Subject + Helping Verb(am/is/are) + Main verb +ing + the rest of the sentence | <ul><li>I am writing a letter to my friend.</li><li>She is studying for her final exams.</li><li>They are watching a movie at the cinema.</li><li>He is cooking dinner in the kitchen.</li></ul> |
| Present Perfect Tense | **Subject + Helping Verb (have/has) + Past participle of the main verb + the rest of the sentence along with the time frame** | <ul><li>I have finished my homework.</li><li>She has visited Paris twice.</li><li>We have already eaten dinner.</li><li>They have just arrived at the airport.</li></ul> |
| Present Perfect Continuous Tense | **Subject + Have/Has + Been + Verb+ ing + the rest of the sentence** | <ul><li>She has been studying English for five years</li><li>They have been working on the project since last month.</li><li>We have been waiting for the bus for over an hour.</li><li>He has been playing the guitar all morning.</li></ul> |

| Tenses | Rules and Formula | Examples |
|---|---|---|
| Simple Past Tense | Subject + Verb + ed / verb in the past tense + the rest of the sentence | • Nupur went to the supermarket yesterday.<br><br>• She walked to the store yesterday.. |
| Past Continuous Tense | Subject + Helping Verb(was/were) + Main verb + ing + the rest of the sentence | • She was studying for her exam all night.<br><br>• They were playing soccer when it started raining. |
| Past Perfect Tense | Subject + Helping Verb (had) + Past participle of the main verb + the rest of the sentence along with the time frame. | • She had finished her homework before the guests arrived.<br><br>• By the time I got to the cinema, the movie had already started. |
| Past Perfect Continuous Tense | Subject + Had + Been + Verb + ing + the rest of the sentence | • He had been drinking milk out the carton when Mom walked into the kitchen.<br><br>• She had been studying for three hours before her friends called her to go out. |

| Tenses | Rules and Formula | Examples |
|---|---|---|
| Simple Future Tense | Subject + will/shall + V1 + Object | - I will travel to Europe next summer.<br>- She will start her new job on Monday. |
| Future Continuous Tense | Subject + will be/shall be + V1 + ing + Object | - At this time tomorrow, I will be studying for my final exams.<br>- By next week, she will be completing her internship. |
| Future Perfect Tense | **Subject + will have/shall have + V3 + Object** | - By the time the guests arrive, we will have cooked dinner<br>- I will have saved enough money to buy a car by the end of the year. |
| Future Perfect Continuous Tense | **Subject + will have been + V1 + ing + Object** | - By the time you arrive, I will have been waiting for two hours<br>- By next summer, they will have been living in their new house for five years. |

# DIRECT AND INDIRECT SPEECH

## Direct Speech:

Direct speech involves quoting the exact words spoken by someone. It is usually enclosed within quotation marks. For example:

- She said, I am going to the store.
- John exclaimed, What a beautiful day!

In direct speech, the speaker's exact words are preserved, including punctuation, tense, and pronouns. It gives a sense of immediacy and can bring the speaker's tone and emotions into the narrative.

## Indirect Speech (Reported Speech):

Indirect speech, also known as reported speech, involves conveying what someone said without quoting their exact words. Instead, the speaker's words are reported in a different form, often using reporting verbs such as said, told, asked, etc. The tense, pronouns, and other elements may change to fit the context. For example:

- She said that she was going to the store.
- John exclaimed that it was a beautiful day.

*Key Differences:

1. **Punctuation**: Direct speech is enclosed within quotation marks, while indirect speech is not.

2. **Tense**: In direct speech, the tense remains unchanged from the original speaker's words, while in indirect speech, the tense may shift depending on the context.

3. **Pronouns**: Pronouns may change in indirect speech to reflect the perspective of the reporting speaker, while in direct speech, the speaker's original pronouns are preserved.

4. **Reporting Verbs**: Reporting verbs like said, told, asked, etc., are often used in indirect speech to introduce the reported speech.

Both direct and indirect speech are important tools in writing and communication, offering different ways to convey what someone said and adding depth to dialogue and narration.

# Changes as per Tense

*In the below table, you can see how tense changes into Indirect speech.*

| Direct Speech | Indirect Speech |
|---|---|
| Present simple (Subject +V1st + Object) | Past simple (Subject +V2 + Object) |
| Present continuous (Subject +is/am/are+V1 +ing+ Object) | Past Continuous (Subject +was/were+V1 +ing+ Object) |
| Present continuous (Subject +is/am/are+V1 +ing+ Object) | Past Continuous (Subject +was/were+V1 +ing+ Object) |
| Present perfect (Subject + has/have+V3+Object) | Past perfect (Subject+had+V3+Object) |
| Past simple (Subject+V2+Object) | Past perfect (Subject+had+V3+Object) |
| Past Continuous (Subject +was/were+V1 +ing+ Object) | Past perfect continuous (Subject +had been+V1 +ing+ Object) |
| Future simple (Subject+ will/shall+V1+object) | Present Conditional (Subject+ would+V1+object) |
| Future Continuous (Subject +will/shall+be+V1 +ing+ Object) | Conditional Continuous (Subject +would+be+V1 +ing+ Object) |

| Direct Speech | Indirect Speech |
|---|---|
| **Can** <br> He said, "I can solve this problem." | **Could** <br> He said that he could solve that problem. |
| **May** <br> He said, "I may go to the park." | **Might** <br> He said that he might go to the park. |
| **Must** <br> He said, "You must complete the project by Friday." | **Had to/ Would have to** <br> He said that I must complete the project by Friday. |
| **Should** <br> She said, "You should work harder." | **Should** <br> She said that I should work harder. |
| **Might** <br> She said, "I might visit my grandma this weekend." | **Might** <br> She said that she might visit her grandma that weekend. |
| **Could** <br> She said, "I could help you with your homework." | **Could** <br> She said that she could help me with my homework. |
| **Will** <br> He said, "I will call you later." | **Would** <br> He said that he would call me later. |
| **Ought to** <br> She said, "You ought to respect your elders." | **Ought to** <br> She said that I ought to respect my elders. |

# ACTIVE VOICE AND PASSIVE VOICE

## Active Voice:
- In active voice, the subject of the sentence performs the action stated by the verb.
- It is straightforward, direct, and usually more engaging for readers.

Example: The cat chased the mouse. (Subject: The cat; Verb: chased; Object: the mouse)

## Passive Voice:
- In passive voice, the subject receives the action expressed by the verb.
- It often obscures the agent performing the action and can make sentences wordy or less direct.

Example: The mouse was chased by the cat. (Subject: The mouse; Verb: was chased; Agent: by the cat)

## Key Differences:

1. **Structure**: Active voice follows a subject-verb-object structure, while passive voice often reverses this order or leaves out the agent entirely.
2. **Clarity**: Active voice is generally clearer and more direct, while passive voice can be ambiguous or vague about who is performing the action.
3. **Engagement**: Active voice tends to be more engaging and dynamic, while passive voice can sound dull or bureaucratic.

**Tips for Choosing:**
- Use active voice for clear and direct communication, especially in persuasive or engaging writing.
- Reserve passive voice for situations where the focus should be on the recipient of the action rather than the actor, or when the actor is unknown or less important.
- Be wary of overusing passive voice, as it can make writing verbose and less engaging.

Here's a brief overview of tenses in both active and passive voice:

## Active Voice:
1. Present Simple: I write.
2. Present Continuous: I am writing.
3. Present Perfect: I have written.
4. Present Perfect Continuous: I have been writing.

5. Past Simple: I wrote.
6. Past Continuous: I was writing.
7. Past Perfect: I had written.
8. Past Perfect Continuous: I had been writing.

9. Future Simple: I will write.
10. Future Continuous: I will be writing.
11. Future Perfect: I will have written.
12. Future Perfect Continuous: I will have been writing.

## Passive Voice:
1. Present Simple: It is written.
2. Present Continuous: It is being written.
3. Present Perfect: It has been written.
4. Present Perfect Continuous: It has been being written.

5. Past Simple: It was written.
6. Past Continuous: It was being written.
7. Past Perfect: It had been written.
8. Past Perfect Continuous: It had been being written.

9. Future Simple: It will be written.
10. Future Continuous: It will be being written.
11. Future Perfect: It will have been written.
12. Future Perfect Continuous: It will have been being written.

In passive voice, the auxiliary verb  to be  is used along with the past participle form of the main verb.

# QUESTION FORMS

Question forms are an essential part of communication. They allow us to gather information, seek clarification, or express curiosity. Common types of question forms include:

1. **Open-ended Questions**
- **Purpose**: Encourage detailed, elaborative responses.
- **Structure**: No fixed answer; invites creativity and expression.
- Example:
  - "What are your thoughts on the impact of climate change on agriculture?"
  - "Can you describe your ideal vacation?"

2. **Close-ended Questions**
- **Purpose**: Seek specific, limited responses, often a "yes" or "no" or one-word answer.
- **Structure**: Focused, narrow in scope.
- Example:
  - "Do you enjoy reading?"
  - "Is the meeting scheduled for 3 PM?"

3. **Factual Questions**
  - **Purpose**: Gather concrete information or facts.
  - **Structure**: Straightforward, focused on accuracy.
  - Example:
  - "What is the capital of France?"
  - "Who invented the telephone?

4. **Hypothetical Questions**
- **Purpose**: Encourage imaginative thinking or problem-solving.
- **Structure**: Based on an imaginary or "what-if" scenario.
- Example:
  - "What would you do if you won the lottery?"
  - "How would the world change if gravity suddenly stopped working?"

## 5. Rhetorical Questions
- **Purpose**: Make a point rather than elicit an answer.
- **Structure**: Often persuasive or dramatic in tone.
- Example:
  - "Isn't it obvious that we need more sustainable energy sources?"
  - "Who wouldn't want to live in a safer world?"

## 6. Leading Questions
- **Purpose**: Influence or guide the respondent toward a particular answer.
- **Structure**: Often implies the desired response.
- Example:
  - "Don't you think this policy is unfair?"
  - "Wouldn't you agree that exercise is essential for health?"

## 7. Probing Questions
- **Purpose**: Encourage deeper thought or clarification.
- **Structure**: Builds on previous responses to dig further.
- Example:
  - "Can you explain why you think that?"
  - "What makes you feel that way?"

## 8. Multiple-choice Questions
- **Purpose**: Offer several options for the respondent to choose from.
- **Structure**: Fixed set of possible answers.
- Example:
  - "What is your favorite season? a) Spring b) Summer c) Fall d) Winter"
  - "Which programming language do you prefer? a) Python b) Java c) C++ d) Other"

## 9. Clarifying Questions
- **Purpose**: Request more information or clear up confusion.
- **Structure**: Directly tied to something previously stated.
- Example:
  - "What do you mean by 'better opportunities'?"
  - "Can you elaborate on the term 'sustainability'?"

# Punctuation

**1. Period (.)**
: Used to end declarative sentences and statements. It's also used in abbreviations.

**2. Comma (,)** : Used to separate items in a list, to separate independent clauses in compound sentences, after introductory phrases, to set off nonessential information, and before conjunctions in compound sentences.

**3. Colon (:)**: Used to introduce a list, explanation, example, or quotation. It can also be used between numbers in time expressions and in ratios.

**4. Semicolon (;)** : Used to join independent clauses that are closely related in meaning, to separate items in a list when the items contain commas, and to separate clauses joined by conjunctive adverbs or transitional phrases.

**5. Question Mark (?)** : Used to end direct questions.

**6. Exclamation Mark (!)** : Used to indicate strong feelings or emotions, to add emphasis, or to convey excitement.

**7. Quotation Marks (     )** : Used to indicate direct speech, to enclose titles of shorter works (e.g., articles, poems), and to indicate irony or sarcasm.

**8. Apostrophe (')** : Used to indicate possession or contraction.

**9. Hyphen (-)** : Used to join compound words, to separate syllables in a word, and to join prefixes and suffixes to root words.

**10. Dash (– or —)** : Used to indicate a sudden change in thought, to set off parenthetical information, or to indicate an interruption in speech.

**11. Parentheses ( )** : Used to enclose additional information that is not essential to the main message but provides clarification or context.

**12. Ellipsis (...)** : Used to indicate omitted words in a quotation, hesitation, or trailing off in thought.

**13. Slash (/)** : Used to indicate alternatives, to separate lines in poetry, or to represent  per  in measurements or abbreviations.

# Punctuation Guide

### Period

Used at the end of a statement

### Exclamation Point

Used to show excitement or emphasis at the end of a sentence

### Question Mark

Used at the end of a question

### Comma

Used to separate phrases or items in a list

### Semicolon

Used to join two independent clauses that are closely related

### Ellipsis

Used to indicate a pause or trailing off of a thought

### Quotation Marks

Used to mark the beginning and end of a quote or to show speech used in a sentence

### Colon

Used to introduce groups of words in a series or introduce a quote

### Apostrophe

Used to show possession

# Synonyms and Antonyms

**Synonyms** are words or phrases that have similar meanings to each other. They provide variety and richness to language, allowing speakers and writers to express themselves more precisely and creatively

**Antonyms** are words that have opposite meanings. They are pairs of words that express contrasting concepts. Understanding antonyms can help in better comprehension, communication, and language enrichment.

| | | |
|---|---|---|
| **Word**: beautiful<br>**Synonym**: gorgeous<br>**Antonym**: hideous | **Word**: hard<br>**Synonym**: tough<br>**Antonym**: soft | **Word**: calm<br>**Synonym**: peaceful<br>**Antonym**: chaotic |
| **Word**: simple<br>**Synonym**: easy<br>**Antonym**: difficult | **Word**: good<br>**Synonym**: nice<br>**Antonym**: bad | **Word**: rich<br>**Synonym**: wealthy<br>**Antonym**: poor |
| **Word**: perfect<br>**Synonym**: ideal<br>**Antonym**: flawed | **Word**: tasty<br>**Synonym**: delicious<br>**Antonym**: revolting | **Word**: stop<br>**Synonym**: pause<br>**Antonym**: go |
| **Word**: tidy<br>**Synonym**: neat<br>**Antonym**: messy | **Word**: nervous<br>**Synonym**: anxious<br>**Antonym**: calm | **Word**: excited<br>**Synonym**: joyful<br>**Antonym**: upset |

# Synonyms

Synonyms are words or phrases that have similar meanings to each other. They provide variety and richness to language, allowing speakers and writers to express themselves more precisely and creatively.

Here are some examples of synonyms with explanations:

1. **Happy / Joyful / Content / Pleased**
·Example: After receiving her exam results, Sarah was happy to see that she had passed with flying colors.

2. **Big / Large / Huge / Enormous**
·Example: The elephant was so big that it could barely fit through the narrow gate.

3. **Angry / Furious / Mad / Irritated**
·Example: John became angry when he realized that someone had taken his parking spot.

4. **Smart / Intelligent / Clever / Bright**
·Example: She proved to be a smart student, always at the top of her class.

5. **Beautiful / Gorgeous / Stunning / Lovely**
·Example: The sunset painted the sky with beautiful hues of orange and pink.

6. **Sad / Unhappy / Miserable / Sorrowful**
·Example: He felt sad when he heard the news of his grandmother's passing.

7. **Funny / Amusing / Hilarious / Entertaining**
·Example: The comedian's jokes were so funny that the entire audience was in stitches.

8. **Difficult / Hard / Challenging / Tough**
·Example: Learning a new language can be difficult, but with practice, it becomes easier.

# SYNONYMS

Synonyms are words that have similar meanings.

fair  balanced

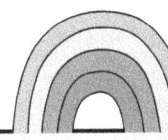 The rainbow is beautiful.
The rainbow is pretty.

# ANTONYMS

Antonyms are words that have opposite meanings.

left  right

She was high.
He was low.

# Antonyms

Antonyms are words that have opposite meanings. They are pairs of words that express contrasting concepts. Understanding antonyms can help in better comprehension, communication, and language enrichment.

Here are some examples of antonyms:

1. **Hot - Cold:**
·Example:    The weather was scorching hot yesterday, but today it's quite cold.
2. **Happy - Sad:**
·Example:    After receiving good news, she felt happy, but the sad news later brought her down.
3. **Light - Dark:**
·Example:    She turned on the light to dispel the darkness in the room.
4. **Fast - Slow:**
·Example:    The cheetah is known for its incredible speed, while the sloth moves at a slow pace.
5. **Big - Small:**
·Example:    The elephant is big, but the mouse is small in comparison.
6. **Up - Down:**
·Example:    He climbed up the stairs to reach the top floor, then later descended back down.
7. **Day - Night:**
·Example:    During the day, the streets are bustling with activity, but at night, they become quiet.
8. **Strong - Weak:**
·Example:    The weightlifter is strong, but the child is weak and needs help lifting heavy objects.

# Homonyms

Homonyms are words that have the same spelling or pronunciation but different meanings. There are two main types of homonyms:

1.**Homographs:** These are words that are spelled the same but have different meanings.
·Example:
1. Bat (a flying mammal) and bat (a piece of sports equipment used in baseball).
2. Bow (a type of knot) and bow (the front part of a ship).
3. Tear (to rip something apart) and tear (a drop of water from the eye).

2.**Homophones**: These are words that sound the same but have different meanings and often different spellings.
·Example:
1. To, two, and too.
2. Bear (the animal) and bare (naked or uncovered).
3. Flour (used in baking) and flower (a bloom).

Homonyms can sometimes create confusion, especially in written communication, so it's important to understand their various meanings in different contexts.

Homophones are words that sound the same but have different meanings and often different spellings. They can be a source of confusion in spoken and written language, especially for learners and those with spelling difficulties.

Here are some examples of homophones:

**1.Their, They're, There:**
·Their: belonging to them (That's their car. )
·They're: contraction of they are ( They're going to the movies. )
·There: indicating a place (The book is over there. )

**2.To, Too, Two:**
·To: indicating direction or action ( I am going to the store. )
·Too: meaning also or excessively ( She wants to come too. )
·Two: the number 2 ( There are two apples on the table. )

## 2. Bear, Bare:
·Bear: a large mammal ( We saw a bear in the woods. )
·Bare: naked or uncovered (The tree branches were bare in winter.)

## 3. Flower, Flour:
·Flower: a plant blossom ( She picked a beautiful flower. )
·Flour: a powder made by grinding grains, used in baking ( We need two cups of flour for the cake. )

## 4. Sea, See:
·Sea: large body of saltwater (We went swimming in the sea. )
·See: to perceive with the eyes ( I can see the mountains from here. )

## 5. Know, No:
·Know: to have information or understanding of something ( I know how to swim. )
·No: a negative response or denial ( No, I haven't seen him. )

## 6. Right, Write:
·Right: correct or opposite of left(Turn right at the next intersection. )
·Write: to inscribe or compose with pen and paper ( Please write your name on the form. )

These examples demonstrate how homophones can sound identical but have different meanings and spellings, which can sometimes lead to confusion in communication.

# Eponyms

Eponyms are words or phrases that derive from the name of a person or a place, usually because that person or place was associated with the concept or item in some significant way. These eponyms can range from everyday objects to medical conditions, and they often serve as a way to honor or remember influential figures.

Here are some examples of eponyms:

1. **Boycott**: This term originated from Charles C. Boycott, an English land agent in Ireland during the late 19th century. His tenants refused to work his land due to unfair treatment, leading to the term boycott to describe the act of refusing to engage in dealings with a person, organization, or country.

2. **Sideburns**: Named after Ambrose Burnside, an American Civil War general known for his distinctive facial hair that extended from his ears to his mustache but did not include a chin beard.

3. **Sandwich**: Named after John Montagu, the 4th Earl of Sandwich, who is reputed to have ordered his meat to be served between two slices of bread so he could eat while playing cards without greasing the cards.

4. **Alzheimer's disease**: Named after Alois Alzheimer, a German psychiatrist and neuropathologist who first identified the condition in 1906 while studying the brain tissue of a deceased patient who had exhibited symptoms of severe memory loss and cognitive decline.

5. **Fahrenheit**: The temperature scale named after Gabriel Fahrenheit, a physicist who invented the mercury-in-glass thermometer and developed the Fahrenheit temperature scale in the early 18th century.

6. **Diesel**: Named after Rudolf Diesel, a German engineer who invented the diesel engine in the late 19th century.

7. **Nicotine**: Named after Jean Nicot, a French ambassador in Portugal during the 16th century, who introduced tobacco to the French court.

8. **Machiavellian**: Derived from Niccolò Machiavelli, an Italian philosopher and writer known for his book   The Prince, which describes the cynical and manipulative strategies used by political leaders.

9. **Cardigan**: Named after James Thomas Brudenell, the 7th Earl of Cardigan, who popularized the style of sweater during the Crimean War.

10. **Platonic**: Named after the ancient Greek philosopher Plato, referring to his teachings on ideal forms and non-romantic relationships based on friendship and intellectual connection.

# Paronyms

Paronyms are words that are similar in sound but have different meanings. These words often create confusion because of their phonetic similarity. However, they are distinct in meaning and usage . Here are some examples of paronyms:

1. **Accept vs. Except:**
·Accept: to receive or agree to something. Example: She accepted the job offer with enthusiasm.
·Except: to exclude or leave out. Example: Everyone is invited to the party except Tom.

2. **Affect vs. Effect:**
·Affect: to influence or have an impact on something. Example: The bad weather affected the crops.
·Effect: the result or consequence of an action. Example: The new law had a significant effect on crime rates.

3. **Advise vs. Advice:**
·Advise: to give guidance or recommend. Example: I advise you to study for the exam.
·Advice: recommendations or guidance given to someone. Example: She gave me some good advice about investing.

4. **Complement vs. Compliment:**
·Complement: something that completes or enhances something else. Example: The red wine was a perfect complement to the steak.
·Compliment: a polite expression of admiration or praise. Example: She received many compliments on her new hairstyle.

5. **Stationary vs. Stationery:**
·Stationary: not moving or still. Example: The car remained stationary at the trafflc llght.
·Stationery: writing materials such as paper, pens, and envelopes.

# Kangaroo words

Kangaroo words are fun linguistic phenomena where a word contains within it a synonym or closely related word. This synonym is often called the "joey," akin to a baby kangaroo riding in its mother's pouch. Essentially, it's a word within a word! The term "kangaroo word" itself is a playful metaphor, likening the way a kangaroo carries its young in its pouch to the way a word carries its "baby" word inside.

Kangaroo words are words that contain within themselves a synonym or definition of the word itself.

Here are five examples:

1. **Preserve (Kangaroo word) - Conserve (Joey word)**
- "Preserve" contains the word "conserve" within it. Both words convey the idea of protecting or maintaining something.

2. **Stable (Kangaroo word) - Able (Joey word)**
- Within "stable" you can find "able." A stable situation often implies being able or capable.

3. **Rehearse (Kangaroo word) - Hear (Joey word)**
- "Rehearse" includes "hear" within it. Rehearsing often involves hearing or listening to something repeatedly.

4. **Dishearten (Kangaroo word) - Sad (Joey word)**
- The word "dishearten" contains "sad" within it. When someone is disheartened, they often feel sad or discouraged.

5. **Subterranean (Kangaroo word) - Terrain (Joey word)**
- "Subterranean" includes "terrain" within it. It refers to something underground or beneath the surface, often relating to terrain or land.

# Diminutives

**Diminutives** are word forms that express smallness, endearment, or familiarity. They are commonly used in many languages to convey a sense of intimacy, cuteness, or affection. In English, diminutives are often formed by adding suffixes like -ie, -y, or -let to the base word, though there are other ways to form diminutives as well.

Here are some examples of diminutives in English:
Diminutives Using Suffixes
1. Booklet (book)
2. Duckling (duck)
3. Piglet (pig)
4. Kitten (cat/kid)
5. Droplet (drop)
6. Leaflet (leaf)
7. Owlet (owl)
8. Streamlet (stream)
9. Lambkin (lamb)
10. Hillock (hill)

These examples demonstrate how diminutives can be formed by adding a suffix, modifying the word, or using a completely different word to convey smallness or endearment.

# Idioms are phrases

Idioms are phrases or expressions that convey a figurative meaning different from the literal interpretation of the individual words. They add color and depth to language and are often deeply rooted in culture. Here are some examples of idioms along with their meanings:

**1. Bite the bullet**
·Meaning: To endure a painful or difficult situation with courage and determination.
·Example: She had to bite the bullet and confront her fear of public speaking during the presentation.

**2. Cost an arm and a leg**
·Meaning: Something is very expensive.
·Example: Buying a new car can cost an arm and a leg, especially if you opt for all the latest features.

**3. Break the ice**
·Meaning: To initiate a conversation or social interaction in order to make people feel more comfortable.
·Example: At the party, Sarah tried to break the ice by telling a funny joke to start the conversation.

**4. Hit the nail on the head**
·Meaning: To describe precisely or accurately what is causing a situation or problem.
·Example: Tom hit the nail on the head when he identified poor communication as the main issue within the team.

**5. Burning the midnight oil**
·Meaning: Working late into the night or staying up late to complete a task.
·Example: With the deadline approaching, the team had to start burning the midnight oil to finish the project on time.

**6. The ball is in your court**
·Meaning: It is now someone else's turn to make a decision or take action.
·Example: I've done everything I can to resolve the issue. Now, the ball is in your court, and you need to decide how to proceed.

7. **Once in a blue moon**
·Meaning: Something that happens very rarely or only occasionally.
·Example: They go on vacation once in a blue moon, so they always make sure it's a memorable trip.

8. **Spill the beans**
·Meaning: To disclose a secret or reveal confidential information.
·Example: Despite their best efforts to keep it a surprise, Sarah accidentally spilled the beans about the party to her brother.

9. **Straight from the horse's mouth**
·Meaning: Information that comes directly from a reliable or authoritative source.
·Example: I heard about the new product launch straight from the horse's mouth – the CEO himself announced it during the meeting.

10. **Under the weather**
·Meaning: Feeling unwell or slightly ill.
·Example: I won't be able to come to work today; I'm feeling a bit under the weather.

Understanding and using idioms can greatly enrich your language skills and help you communicate more effectively, but it's important to remember that idioms can be culturally specific and their meanings may not always be immediately obvious to non-native speakers.

Here are some more idioms and phrases;

1. **A piece of cake**: Something very easy.
2. **Actions speak louder than words**: What you do is more important than what you say.
3. **All ears**: Fully listening or eager to hear.
4. **Bite the bullet**: To endure a painful experience or face a difficult situation courageously.
5. **Break the ice**: To initiate a conversation or activity to relax tension or formality.
6. **Burning the midnight oil**: Working late into the night.
7. **Cost an arm and a leg**: Extremely expensive.

8. **Cry over spilled milk**: To regret something that has already happened.

9. **Cut to the chase**: Skip the preliminaries and get to the main point.

10. **Down to the wire:** Reaching the last minute or seconds.

11. **Easier said than done:** Something that appears simple but is actually quite difficult to accomplish.

12. **Every cloud has a silver lining:** There's something positive in every negative situation.

13. **Hit the nail on the head:** To describe exactly what is causing a situation or problem.

14. **Jump on the bandwagon**: To join a popular trend or activity.

15. **Kick the bucket**: Euphemism for dying.

16. **Kill two birds with one stone:** Accomplish two things with a single action.

17. **Let the cat out of the bag:** To reveal a secret.

18. **Miss the boat**: To miss an opportunity.

19. **On the ball**: Alert, competent, or skillful.

20. **Piece of cake:** A task or activity that is very easy.

21. **Pull someone's leg**: To tease or joke with someone.

22.. **Rain cats and dogs**: To rain heavily.

23. **Saved by the bell:** Rescued from an undesirable situation by a timely interruption.

24. **Spill the beans**: To reveal a secret or information that should be kept confidential.

25. **Steal someone's thunder**: To take credit for someone else's achievements or ideas.

26. **Take the bull by the horns**: To confront a difficult situation head-on.

27. **The ball is in your court:** It's your turn to make a decision or take action.

28. **Throw in the towel:** To give up or surrender.
29. **Under the weather**: Feeling unwell or sick.
30. **Up in the air:** Uncertain or undecided.
31. **Vanishing act**: Disappearing suddenly or without explanation.
32. **Walking on thin ice:** Engaging in risky behavior or being in a precarious situation.
33. **Wild goose chase:** A futile pursuit or search.
34. **You can't judge a book by its cover**: You cannot accurately judge someone or something based solely on appearance.
35. **Zip one's lips**: To remain silent or keep a secret.
36. **Back to the drawing board**: When a plan or project fails and it's time to start over.
37. **Burn bridges:** To damage relationships or opportunities beyond repair.
38. **Get cold feet**: To feel nervous or anxious about something that was previously planned or decided.
39. **Give someone the cold shoulder:** To ignore or treat someone with disdain.
40. **Hit the hay:** To go to bed or go to sleep.

## 1.  **Phrase**:

A phrase is a group of words that function together as a single unit within a sentence, but it does not contain both a subject and a verb (predicate). Phrases can serve different purposes in a sentence, such as functioning as nouns, verbs, adjectives, or adverbs. For example:
· The big, blue house (noun phrase)
· Running swiftly (verb phrase)
· Very quickly (adverb phrase)
· Extremely talented (adjective phrase)

## 2. **Clause**:

A clause is a group of words that contains both a subject and a predicate (verb), and it can function as a complete sentence or as part of a larger sentence. There are two main types of clauses: independent clauses and dependent clauses.

- **Independent Clause:** It can stand alone as a complete sentence because it expresses a complete thought. For example: She went to the store.
- **Dependent Clause:** It cannot stand alone as a complete sentence because it does not express a complete thought. Dependent clauses are often introduced by subordinating conjunctions like because, although, when, etc. For example: Because she was hungry, she went to the store.

2. **Sentence:** A sentence is a group of words that expresses a complete thought. It contains a subject, a verb, and often, an object. Sentences can vary in length and complexity. They can be simple, compound, complex, or compound-complex.
- **Simple Sentence:** It contains one independent clause. For example: I like to read.
- **Compound Sentence**: It contains two or more independent clauses joined by coordinating conjunctions (such as and, but, or, etc.) or by semicolons. For example: She likes to read, but he prefers to watch movies.
- **Complex Sentence**: It contains one independent clause and one or more dependent clauses. For example: Although she likes to read, she doesn't have much free time.
- **Compound-Complex Sentence**: It contains two or more independent clauses and one or more dependent clauses. For example: She enjoys reading, but when she's busy, she listens to audiobooks while doing chores.

## Key Difference: Phrase vs. Clause

- A phrase cannot stand alone as a complete sentence; it provides additional information.
- A clause can be independent and stand alone as a complete sentence or dependent when attached to another clause.

# Composition

In grammar, composition refers to the way in which words, phrases, and clauses are organized and combined to create sentences and larger units of discourse, such as paragraphs and essays. Composition encompasses various elements, including sentence structure, word order, punctuation, and coherence, all of which contribute to the clarity and effectiveness of written communication.

Effective composition involves:

- **Sentence Structure:** This refers to how sentences are constructed, including the arrangement of subject, verb, and object, as well as the use of modifiers, clauses, and phrases.
- **Word Choice**: The selection of appropriate words and vocabulary to convey the intended meaning accurately and precisely.
- **Punctuation**: The use of punctuation marks such as commas, periods, semicolons, and dashes to clarify the meaning and structure of sentences.
- .**Coherence and Unity**: Ensuring that ideas are logically connected and that there is a clear progression of thought throughout the text.
- .**Paragraph Structure:** The organization of ideas into coherent paragraphs, each with a main idea supported by relevant details and examples.
- **Transitions:** Using transitional words and phrases to smoothly connect different parts of the composition and guide the reader through the text.
- **Style and Tone:** The overall manner in which the writing is presented, including the author's voice, attitude, and level of formality.

By paying attention to these aspects of composition, writers can create clear, engaging, and effective communication that effectively conveys their intended message.

# Letter Writing

In grammar, letter writing refers to the art and skill of composing written messages in the form of letters. It involves following certain conventions and formats to effectively communicate ideas, thoughts, requests, or information in a written format. Letter writing can take various forms and serve different purposes depending on the context and audience. Here are the types of letter writing commonly encountered:

- **Formal Letters:** These are written for official or professional purposes. They follow a specific format and language conventions. Examples include letters of application, resignation letters, complaint letters, business letters, and letters to officials or authorities.
- **Informal Letters**: Also known as personal letters, these are written to friends, family members, or acquaintances. They are more casual in tone and format compared to formal letters. Informal letters may include personal anecdotes, updates on life events, or casual conversations.
- **Business Letters:** These are formal letters exchanged within a business context. They can include letters of inquiry, letters of recommendation, sales letters, and letters of introduction. Business letters typically adhere to specific formatting guidelines and use professional language.
- **Cover Letters**: Cover letters accompany job applications and provide an introduction to the applicant, highlighting relevant skills, experiences, and motivations for applying for a particular position. They are tailored to the job and company to which the application is being submitted.
- **Personal Letters**: These are informal letters written for personal communication. They may include letters to friends, family members, pen pals, or romantic partners. Personal letters allow individuals to express emotions, share experiences, or maintain connections with loved ones.
- **Official Letters**: Official letters are written to communicate with government agencies, institutions, or organizations. Examples include letters to government officials, letters of complaint to companies, or letters to academic institutions.
- **Circular Letters:** These letters are sent to a large number of recipients simultaneously. They may be used for announcements, invitations, or general communication within an organization or community.

8. **Application Letters**: These letters are written to apply for a job, admission to an educational institution, or participation in a program or event. They highlight the applicant's qualifications, interests, and suitability for the position or opportunity.

These are some of the common types of letter writing, each serving a specific purpose and following distinct conventions in terms of format, tone, and content.

Letter writing typically consists of several key parts, each serving a specific purpose. Here's a breakdown of the common parts of a letter:

**1. Sender's Address:** Your address should be placed at the top right-hand corner of the page. This includes your name, street address, city, state, and ZIP code.

**2. Date:** The date should be placed below your address, aligned with the left margin. It's usually written in full, for example, April 4, 2024.

**3. Recipient's Address:** The recipient's address should follow the date, aligned with the left margin. Include the recipient's name, title (if applicable), company or organization name, street address, city, state, and ZIP code.

**4. Salutation:** Begin your letter with a greeting, such as Dear [Recipient's Name], or to Whom It May Concern, depending on your level of familiarity with the recipient and the formality of the letter.

**5. Body**: The body of the letter contains the main message you wish to convey. It's important to be clear, concise, and organized in your writing. Break up the text into paragraphs for readability and structure.

**6. Closing:** End your letter with a closing remark or statement, such as Sincerely, Best regards, or Yours faithfully, followed by a comma. The choice of closing depends on the level of formality and your relationship with the recipient.

**7. Signature:** Leave space between the closing and your typed name to sign the letter by hand if it's being sent via traditional mail. If the letter is being sent electronically, you can include a scanned version of your signature or simply type your name below the closing.

8. **Postscript (optional):** If you have an additional comment or message to add after you've finished the letter, you can include a postscript below your signature. This is often abbreviated as P.S. and is preceded by a colon. Remember to proofread your letter carefully before sending it to ensure that it's error-free and effectively communicates your intended message. Additionally, tailor the tone and style of your letter to suit the purpose and audience, whether it's formal, informal, professional, or personal.

## Difference between Formal and Informal Letter

| Formal Letter | Informal Letter |
|---|---|
| It is written in a formal way or a professional way. | It can be casual also. |
| It is an official announcement by a person or a firm. | It is non-official. |
| The format of the letter should be followed. | There is no particular format. |
| They are written for official reasons. | They are written for personal reasons. |

# Formal Letter
## Example of a School Leave Application

[Your Name]
[Your Address]
[City, State, ZIP Code]
[Date]

The Principal
[School Name]
[School Address]
[City, State, ZIP Code]

Subject: Application for Leave

Respected Sir/Madam,

    I am writing to request leave for [number of days] from [start date] to [end date] as I [state reason, e.g., am unwell, have a family event, or need to travel]. I kindly request you to grant me permission to be absent from school during this period.
    I assure you that I will complete all pending assignments and catch up on any missed lessons upon my return.
I kindly request your approval for my leave application. Please let me know if any further details or documentation are required.
Thank you for your consideration.

Yours obediently,
[Your Full Name]
[Class and Section]
[Roll Number]

# Informal Letter

[Your Address]
[City, State, ZIP Code]
[Date]

Dear [Recipient's Name],

[Opening paragraph: Start by asking about the recipient's well-being or sharing something casual to set a friendly tone. Mention why you're writing the letter.]

[Main body paragraphs: Share your news, updates, or details about the subject of the letter. This section can include personal experiences, anecdotes, or questions to engage the recipient. Keep the tone conversational and warm.]

[Closing paragraph: Conclude by expressing your hopes, wishes, or plans to meet soon. Mention any specific request or action if needed, and convey your affection or regards.]

Yours lovingly/affectionately,
[Your Name]


**Example**

123 Rosewood Lane
Chennai, Tamil Nadu 600001
December 9, 2024

Dear Priya,

    How are you? I hope this letter finds you happy and healthy. It's been such a long time since we've had a proper chat, and I thought of writing to you to catch up on everything that's been happening in our lives.

    Things here have been quite busy but exciting! Last week, we went on a family trip to Ooty, and it was amazing. The weather was perfect, and we visited some beautiful tea estates. I kept thinking about how much fun we would've had if you were with us! How's school going for you? I heard from Aunt that you scored really well in your exams—congratulations!

    I really miss the times we spent during the holidays, playing games and staying up late talking. Let's plan to meet during the next break—I'll convince Mom and Dad to visit you in Bangalore. We can explore the city and have so much fun together! Take care of yourself and do write back when you get the chance. Give my love to Uncle and Aunt. I can't wait to hear from you!

Yours lovingly,
Rohan

# Essay

An essay is a piece of writing that presents an argument, analysis, or discussion on a particular topic. It is typically structured and organized with a clear introduction, body paragraphs, and a conclusion. Essays can vary in length from short pieces of a few paragraphs to longer, more in-depth works.

There are several types of essays, each with its own unique purpose and structure:

1. **Descriptive Essay**: This type of essay aims to provide a detailed description of a person, place, object, or event. It often appeals to the senses and paints a vivid picture for the reader.
2. **Narrative Essay**: In a narrative essay, the writer tells a story or recounts a series of events. This type of essay often includes personal anecdotes and can be used to illustrate a point or convey a message.
3. **Expository Essay:** Expository essays aim to explain or inform the reader about a particular topic. They present facts, statistics, and examples to support their arguments and often include definitions and explanations of terms.
4. **Persuasive Essay:** Also known as an argumentative essay, a persuasive essay aims to convince the reader to adopt the writer's point of view or take a particular action. It presents arguments supported by evidence and often includes counterarguments to address opposing viewpoints.
5. **Compare and Contrast Essay**: This type of essay examines the similarities and differences between two or more subjects. It typically presents a thesis statement that highlights the main points of comparison and contrast, followed by detailed analysis in the body paragraphs.
6. **Cause and Effect Essay**: Cause and effect essays explore the relationship between events or phenomena, discussing how one event leads to another or how multiple factors contribute to a particular outcome.

7. **Analytical Essay**: Analytical essays analyze a piece of literature, film, artwork, or other media. They often focus on themes, characters, symbolism, or other elements to uncover deeper meanings and interpretations.

8. **Argumentative Essay**: Similar to persuasive essays, argumentative essays present a claim or thesis statement and provide evidence to support it. However, argumentative essays tend to be more research-based and rely heavily on logical reasoning and factual evidence.

These are some of the most common types of essays, but there are many other variations and hybrids as well. The type of essay you write will depend on the purpose, audience, and requirements of the assignment.

Here are some general hints to help you with your essay:

1. **Understand the Prompt**: Make sure you thoroughly understand the essay prompt or question before you start writing. Highlight or underline key phrases to ensure you stay focused on what's being asked.
2. **Brainstorm Ideas:** Take some time to brainstorm potential points, arguments, or examples that you could include in your essay. Jot down any relevant information or connections that come to mind.
3. **Create an Outline**: Organize your thoughts by creating an outline for your essay. This will help you structure your writing and ensure that you cover all necessary points. Include an introduction, body paragraphs, and a conclusion.
4. **Craft a Strong Thesis Statement:** Your thesis statement should clearly articulate the main argument or purpose of your essay. It sets the tone for the entire piece and guides the reader on what to expect.
5. **Use Clear and Concise Language**: Aim for clarity and simplicity in your writing. Avoid using overly complex language or jargon that might confuse your readers. Be concise and get straight to the point.
6. **Provide Evidence and Examples**: Back up your arguments with evidence and examples. This could include statistics, research findings, quotations, or anecdotes that support your claims and add credibility to your writing.
7. **Address Counterarguments:** Anticipate potential counterarguments to your thesis and address them within your essay. Acknowledging opposing viewpoints demonstrates critical thinking and strengthens your overall argument.

8. **Stay Organized and Cohesive:** Ensure that your essay flows logically from one point to the next. Use transitional phrases and clear topic sentences to guide your reader through your argument.

9. **Revise and Edit**: Once you've written a draft of your essay, take the time to revise and edit it carefully. Look for grammar and spelling errors, as well as opportunities to improve clarity, coherence, and overall quality.

10. **Seek Feedback:** Consider sharing your essay with a peer, teacher, or tutor for feedback. Fresh perspectives can help you identify areas for improvement and refine your writing further.

Remember to tailor these hints to the specific requirements of your essay assignment and to your own writing style and preferences.

An essay typically consists of several key parts that work together to convey a coherent message or argument. Here are the essential components of an essay:

1. **Introduction**: This is the beginning of the essay where you introduce the topic to the reader. The introduction should provide background information, context, and often includes a thesis statement—a concise summary of the main point or argument of the essay. The introduction should also grab the reader's attention and set the tone for the rest of the essay.
   - Hook: A compelling opening statement to grab the reader's attention.
   - Background Information: Brief context or overview of the topic.
   - Thesis Statement: A clear, concise statement that outlines the main argument or purpose of the essay.

2. **Thesis Statement**: As mentioned above, the thesis statement is a crucial element of the introduction. It states the main argument or purpose of the essay and guides the reader on what to expect in the following paragraphs. A strong thesis statement is clear, specific, and debatable.

3. **Body Paragraphs:** The body of the essay consists of one or more paragraphs that support and develop the main argument presented in the thesis statement. Each body paragraph should focus on a single main idea or aspect of the argument and provide evidence, examples, or analysis to support it. Transitional sentences are often used to smoothly connect one paragraph to the next and maintain the flow of the essay.

4. **Topic Sentences**: Each body paragraph typically begins with a topic sentence that introduces the main idea or point of that paragraph. The topic sentence acts as a preview of the information to come and helps maintain the organization and coherence of the essay.

5. **Supporting Evidence**: Throughout the body paragraphs, it's important to include relevant evidence to support the main argument. This evidence can come from various sources, such as scholarly articles, books, statistics, personal experiences, or observations. It's crucial to properly cite any sources used and to ensure that the evidence is credible and effectively reinforces the argument.

6. **Analysis and Interpretation:** Alongside presenting evidence, it's essential to analyze and interpret the evidence to demonstrate its significance and relevance to the main argument. Analysis involves examining the evidence critically, discussing its implications, and explaining how it supports the thesis statement.

7. **Counterarguments and Refutation (optional):** In some essays, it's important to acknowledge opposing viewpoints or counterarguments and refute them. This demonstrates a thorough understanding of the topic and strengthens the overall argument by addressing potential objections or criticisms.

8. **Conclusion**: The conclusion is the final part of the essay where you summarize the main points and restate the thesis statement in a fresh way. It should provide closure to the essay and leave a lasting impression on the reader. Additionally, the conclusion may offer insights, implications, or suggestions for further research related to the topic.

9. **Closing Statement or Call to Action (optional):** In some cases, essays may end with a closing statement that reinforces the main argument or encourages the reader to take action or further explore the topic.

Overall, these parts work together to create a well-structured and persuasive essay that effectively communicates ideas and arguments to the reader.

Here are some essay topics across various subjects:

1. **Literature**:
· Analyze the role of symbolism in The Great Gatsby by F. Scott Fitzgerald.
· Compare and contrast the themes of love and betrayal in Shakespeare's Romeo and Juliet and Othello.

2. **History**:
· Evaluate the impact of the Industrial Revolution on society and the economy.
· Analyze the causes and consequences of the American Civil War.

3. **Science:**
· Explore the ethical implications of genetic engineering and gene editing technologies.
· Discuss the potential benefits and risks of artificial intelligence in society.

4. **Philosophy**:
· Examine the concept of justice in Plato's Republic.
· Discuss the meaning of life from existentialist perspectives.
· Analyze the ethical theories of utilitarianism and deontology in moral decision-making.

5. **Sociology:**
Investigate the relationship between social media usage and mental health among adolescents. ·Examine the phenomenon of income inequality and its impact on society. ·Analyze the role of gender stereotypes in shaping societal expectations and norms.

6. **Psychology:**
Discuss the nature vs. nurture debate in human development. ·Explore the psychology of addiction and its effects on individuals and society. ·Analyze the factors influencing conformity and obedience in social psychology.

7. **Politics:**
Evaluate the impact of globalization on national sovereignty. ·Discuss the role of political ideologies in shaping modern governance. ·Analyze the challenges and opportunities of multiculturalism in contemporary democracies.

Remember, when writing essays, it's crucial to clearly state your thesis, provide evidence to support your arguments, and engage critically with the topic. Additionally, ensure that your essay follows a coherent structure with well-developed paragraphs and a logical flow of ideas.

# 1. Descriptive Essay: "A Day at the Beach"

Title: A Day at the Beach

The sun rose lazily over the horizon, casting a warm golden glow over the ocean. As I walked along the shore, the soft sand squished beneath my feet, cool and comforting after the morning dew. The air was thick with the scent of saltwater, and I could hear the gentle lapping of waves against the shore. The beach was alive with the sounds of seagulls calling out, the rustle of palm trees swaying in the breeze, and the distant laughter of children playing in the surf.

I made my way to the water, feeling the cool waves crash against my ankles. The water, clear and sparkling, danced under the sunlight. It was refreshing, a perfect balance between coolness and warmth. As I waded deeper, I marveled at the small fish darting past my feet, and I smiled, realizing how peaceful this simple moment was.

By noon, the beach had filled with people, but it never felt crowded. People lounged under umbrellas, reading books or chatting with friends. Others played volleyball or surfed the waves, their joyful shouts mixing with the sound of the ocean. The entire scene felt like a perfect escape from the busy world.

As the day turned to evening, the sky transformed into a canvas of oranges, pinks, and purples, reflecting on the calm water. I sat on the sand, watching the sunset, feeling content and connected to the world around me. The peaceful rhythm of the waves and the beauty of the moment reminded me of the simple joys of life.

# 2. Argumentative Essay: "The Importance of Renewable Energy"

Title: The Importance of Renewable Energy for a Sustainable Future

In the face of climate change and environmental degradation, the transition from fossil fuels to renewable energy sources is not just a possibility but a necessity. Renewable energy—such as solar, wind, and hydropower—presents a sustainable alternative to the finite and polluting fossil fuels that have been the cornerstone of global energy for centuries. This essay argues that renewable energy is crucial for reducing carbon emissions, ensuring energy security, and creating a sustainable future.

One of the most compelling reasons to invest in renewable energy is its potential to reduce carbon emissions. Fossil fuels are the primary contributors to greenhouse gas emissions, which are driving climate change. According to the Intergovernmental Panel on Climate Change (IPCC), reducing emissions by transitioning to renewable energy is essential to limit global warming to 1.5 degrees Celsius. Solar and wind energy, for example, produce little to no carbon dioxide during operation, making them crucial to mitigating climate change.

In addition to environmental benefits, renewable energy also contributes to energy security. Unlike fossil fuels, which are concentrated in a few regions and subject to volatile prices and geopolitical tensions, renewable energy sources are abundant and can be harnessed locally. This reduces dependency on foreign energy imports, improves energy independence, and can help stabilize national economies.

In conclusion, renewable energy is critical for reducing carbon emissions, ensuring energy security, and building a sustainable future. Governments and individuals alike must prioritize the development and implementation of renewable energy technologies to combat climate change, reduce reliance on finite resources, and create a more sustainable world for future generations.

## 3. Expository Essay: "The Role of Education in Personal Development"

**Title**: The Role of Education in Personal Development

Education is often regarded as the key to personal growth, offering individuals the tools and knowledge necessary to achieve their goals and live fulfilling lives. While the traditional view of education focuses on academic achievement, its impact extends far beyond the classroom. Education plays a crucial role in shaping one's character, worldview, and ability to contribute meaningfully to society.

One of the most significant ways education influences personal development is by fostering critical thinking skills. Through exposure to various subjects, ideas, and perspectives, students learn how to analyze information, evaluate different viewpoints, and make informed decisions. These skills are not only valuable in academic settings but are also essential for navigating the complexities of everyday life, from solving problems to making ethical choices.

In addition to cognitive growth, education also promotes emotional and social development. Schools and universities are environments where individuals interact with people from diverse backgrounds, fostering empathy, communication, and collaboration. These interpersonal skills are crucial for personal relationships and professional success. Education also provides opportunities for self-discovery, helping individuals identify their interests, strengths, and passions, which guide career choices and personal goals. Furthermore, education provides individuals with the knowledge and skills to contribute to their communities and society. It empowers people to advocate for positive change, participate in civic duties, and pursue careers that make a difference. Whether it's through teaching, healthcare, or technology, education enables individuals to use their talents to improve the world around them.

In conclusion, education plays a vital role in personal development by fostering intellectual, emotional, and social growth. It shapes individuals into well-rounded, capable, and compassionate people who can make meaningful contributions to society. As such, education should be recognized as an essential foundation for personal and collective progress.

4. **Narrative Essay:** "A Life-Changing Experience"

Title: A Life-Changing Experience

It was a quiet Saturday afternoon when I received the phone call that would change my life forever. I had been volunteering at a local animal shelter for several months, and that day, they called to let me know they had a dog in desperate need of a home. The dog was a young, scared terrier who had been rescued from an abusive situation. It was clear that he needed love and patience to heal, and somehow, I knew that I was the one who could help him.

I arrived at the shelter that evening, heart pounding with excitement and nerves. When I saw him, his eyes were wide with fear, and he trembled as I knelt down to greet him. He had clearly been through so much, but there was a spark of hope in his eyes. I took a deep breath and gently offered my hand. To my surprise, he cautiously approached me and sniffed my fingers, as though sensing that I wasn't there to hurt him. It was in that moment that I knew our lives were about to change.

Taking him home was not easy. There were days when he would hide under the furniture or refuse to eat, but little by little, I gained his trust. We spent hours together, walking through the park, playing fetch, and simply being in each other's company. Over time, he blossomed into a playful, loving companion. His transformation was incredible, and I realized that my life had also changed in ways I hadn't anticipated.

This experience taught me the importance of patience, compassion, and the profound connection between humans and animals. It showed me that sometimes, the smallest gestures can make the biggest difference, and that love and care can heal even the most broken souls.

# Precis

**Precis** writing is the process of condensing a passage to its essential meaning, conveying the main ideas while maintaining the original tone and intent of the author. It requires a deep understanding of the text and the ability to express its core message concisely and accurately.

Here are the steps typically involved in writing a precis:

**1.Read the passage thoroughly:** Understand the main ideas, arguments, and supporting details presented in the passage. Highlight or take notes on key points.

**2.Identify the main theme**: Determine the central idea or theme of the passage. This will guide you in deciding which information is essential to include in the precis.

**3.Summarize the main points**: Write a brief summary of the passage, focusing on the most important ideas and arguments. Exclude any unnecessary details or examples.

**4.Understand the tone and style:** Pay attention to the author's tone and writing style. Your precis should reflect the original tone while being concise and clear.

**5.Compose the precis:** Write the precis in your own words, maintaining the structure and coherence of the original passage. Use simple and straightforward language, avoiding unnecessary embellishments.

**6.Review and revise**: After writing the precis, review it carefully to ensure that it accurately reflects the main ideas of the passage. Edit for clarity, coherence, and conciseness.

**7.Check for accuracy**: Verify that the precis captures the essence of the original passage without distorting its meaning. Make any necessary adjustments to ensure accuracy.

**8..Ensure proper formatting:** Format the precis according to the guidelines provided, if any.

Writing a precis involves condensing and summarizing a larger piece of text while retaining its key points and main ideas.

Here are the essential parts of precis writing:

1. **Title**: Provide a concise title that captures the essence of the original text.
2. **Author's Name:** Include the name of the author of the original text.
3. **Introduction:** Introduce the original text briefly, including its title, author, and the main topic or argument.
4. **Thesis Statement:** Summarize the main argument or central idea of the original text in one or two sentences.
5. **Summary**: Provide a condensed version of the original text, focusing on the main points, arguments, and supporting evidence. Eliminate unnecessary details, examples, and repetitions.
6. **Paraphrasing:** Restate the ideas of the original text in your own words while maintaining clarity and accuracy.
7. **Logical Structure:** Organize the precis in a logical manner, following the structure of the original text. Use transitional words and phrases to connect ideas smoothly.
8. **Length**: Keep the precis concise, typically aiming for about one-third to one-fourth of the length of the original text.
9. **Clarity and Coherence:** Ensure that the precis is clear, coherent, and easy to understand. Use precise language and avoid ambiguity.
10. **Proofreading:** Carefully review the precis for grammar, punctuation, and spelling errors. Make any necessary revisions to improve clarity and readability.

**Example** :

**Original Passage:**

Modern civilization is dominated by science. Its influence is everywhere, shaping our thoughts, lifestyles, and even social institutions. From the moment we wake up, we are surrounded by scientific inventions. The electric light, the fan, the telephone, and the vehicle we use to commute are all products of science. However, science is not limited to practical applications. It also fosters curiosity and expands human knowledge. While science has provided countless benefits, its misuse has led to problems such as pollution and weapons of destruction. It is essential to use scientific advancements responsibly for the betterment of humanity.

**Detailed Précis:**

**Title: The Role of Science in Modern Life**
**Précis:**
Science dominates modern civilization, influencing thoughts, lifestyles, and institutions. Everyday conveniences such as lights, fans, telephones, and vehicles are results of scientific inventions. Beyond practical uses, science encourages curiosity and expands human knowledge. However, the misuse of science has caused issues like pollution and destructive weapons. To ensure progress, science must be used responsibly for the welfare of humanity.

This example includes a title and summarizes the key ideas of the original passage while omitting unnecessary elaborations or examples. The précis conveys the essence of the passage concisely and retains its original meaning.

# Example :

**Original Passage:**
Education is the foundation of personal and societal development. It opens doors to opportunities, broadens perspectives, and empowers individuals to make informed decisions. Through education, people gain knowledge, skills, and values that help them contribute to their communities and the world at large. However, access to quality education remains unequal, with many underprivileged groups being left behind. Addressing this disparity requires collective efforts from governments, organizations, and individuals. By ensuring equal access to education, societies can work towards reducing inequality and fostering progress.

**Detailed Précis:**

**Title: The Importance of Education and Equal Access**
**Précis:**
Education is crucial for personal growth and societal progress, offering knowledge, skills, and values that enable individuals to contribute positively. It fosters opportunities and informed decision-making. However, unequal access to quality education remains a challenge, particularly for underprivileged groups. Collective efforts from governments, organizations, and individuals are needed to address this disparity. Equal access to education is essential for reducing inequality and advancing society.

This précis captures the essence of the passage, maintaining clarity, conciseness, and coherence while presenting the key points.

# Paraphrase

Paraphrase writing involves expressing the meaning of a sentence, passage, or text in your own words, while retaining the original idea. It requires altering the wording and structure without changing the intent or meaning of the original content. Paraphrasing is a critical skill for writing summaries, analyses, and essays, and helps to avoid plagiarism.

Example of Paraphrasing with a Famous Poem
Let's take the first stanza of William Wordsworth's famous poem "I Wandered Lonely as a Cloud":
Original Text:

> I wandered lonely as a cloud
> That floats on high o'er vales and hills,
> When all at once I saw a crowd,
> A host, of golden daffodils;
> Beside the lake, beneath the trees,
> Fluttering and dancing in the breeze.

Paraphrased Version:
I strolled alone, much like a solitary cloud drifting over valleys and hills. Suddenly, I came across a large group of golden daffodils growing by the lake and under the trees, swaying and moving gracefully in the wind.

Key Steps in Paraphrasing Poetry:
1. Understand the Poem's Meaning: Read carefully to capture the essence of the poem's imagery, tone, and message.
2. Simplify the Language: Use modern or simpler words to convey the same ideas.
3. Preserve the Original Emotion: While rewording, maintain the feelings or mood of the poem.
4. Avoid Direct Copying: Refrain from using the poet's exact phrasing unless quoting.

Paraphrasing allows readers to interpret complex poetic language in a way that's accessible and understandable while appreciating the poet's original intent.

# Office note

An office note typically refers to a written record or documentation of activities, discussions, decisions, or observations made during a meeting, appointment, or any other work-related interaction in an office setting. Office notes can vary widely in format and content depending on the purpose and context of the communication. They are often used for internal communication, reference, and documentation within an organization to keep track of important information and actions taken. Office notes can be handwritten or typed and may include details such as meeting agendas, key points discussed, action items assigned, and follow-up tasks. They serve as a tool for maintaining transparency, accountability, and continuity in workplace communication and collaboration.

Here are some examples of office notes:

1. **Meeting Summary Note**: After a team meeting, a note might be written summarizing key points discussed, decisions made, and action items assigned to various team members.

2. **Progress Update Note:** A note documenting the progress of a project, including milestones achieved, challenges faced, and next steps planned.

3. **Action Item Note:** A note listing specific tasks assigned to individuals or teams, along with deadlines and any relevant details.

4. **Decision Log Note:** A note documenting important decisions made within a project or organization, along with the rationale behind each decision and any potential implications.

5. **Training Session Note:** Notes taken during a training session, workshop, or seminar, outlining key concepts, tips, and strategies discussed for future reference.

6 **Client Interaction Note**: A note summarizing a client meeting or conversation, including client requirements, feedback, and any follow-up actions required.

7. **Problem-Solving Note:** A note documenting the steps taken to address a particular problem or issue, including analysis, proposed solutions, and outcomes.

8. **Feedback Note**: A note providing feedback to employees or team members, highlighting areas of strength, areas for improvement, and suggestions for development.

9. **Policy Change Note:** A note informing employees about changes to company policies, procedures, or guidelines, along with explanations for the changes and any implications for the team.

10 **Brainstorming Session Note:** Notes taken during a brainstorming session, capturing ideas generated, potential strategies, and any action plans developed as a result.

**Office Note - Acknowledgement of Receipt**

Date: November 24, 2024
To: Emily White, Marketing Team
From: Mark Lee, Finance Team
Subject: Acknowledgment of Budget Report Submission

Dear Emily,

 I would like to acknowledge the receipt of the updated budget report for the upcoming marketing campaign. I will review the details and provide any necessary feedback by the end of the week.

Thank you for your timely submission.

Best regards,
Mark Lee
Finance Team


**Office Note - Internal Notification of New Policy**

Date: November 24, 2024
To: All Employees
From: HR Department
Subject: New Remote Work Policy Implementation

Dear All,

 We are pleased to announce that a new Remote Work Policy will be implemented starting December 1, 2024. This policy allows eligible employees to work from home two days a week. Please refer to the detailed guidelines attached and reach out to HR with any questions or clarifications.

We believe this new policy will provide more flexibility while maintaining productivity.

Best regards,
HR Department

## Meeting Summary - Project Update Meeting

Date: November 24, 2024
Time: 10:00 AM - 11:00 AM
Location: Conference Room A / Virtual

**Attendees: John Smith, Emily White, Mark Lee, Sarah Black**

Apologies: None

Agenda:
1. Project Timeline Updates
2. Budget Review
3. Marketing Strategy
4. Any Other Business (AOB)

**Meeting Discussion:**
1. Project Timeline Updates:
    - John provided an update on the current project status.
    - Task completion rate stands at 70%. The development team has completed phase 1, and phase 2 is scheduled to begin next week.
2. Budget Review:
    - Mark presented the updated budget, highlighting an unexpected increase in material costs.
    - It was agreed to explore cost-saving measures by reducing unnecessary overhead costs.
3. Marketing Strategy:
    - Emily shared the marketing team's proposed strategy for product launch.
    - Plans include digital advertising, influencer partnerships, and email campaigns.
    - The team agreed to review and finalize marketing content by next meeting.
4. AOB:
    - John raised the topic of potential team expansion. Sarah and Mark to provide a recruitment plan by the next meeting.
    - Next meeting scheduled for December 1, 2024, to finalize the revised budget and marketing strategy.

**Action Items:**
- John to update the project plan for phase 2 by November 28.
- Emily to finalize the marketing content by December 1.
- Mark to prepare a budget revision proposal by November 30.
- Sarah to draft a recruitment plan by December 1.

Meeting Adjourned: 11:00 AM
Next Meeting: December 1, 2024, at 10:00 AM

A memo, short for memorandum, is a concise written message used within an organization for communication. Memos are typically used for conveying important information, announcing changes, providing updates, issuing reminders, or making requests. They are commonly circulated among employees or departments within a company. Here's an explanation of what a memo typically includes,

**Header**: A memo usually begins with a header that includes the following elements:
·To: (Recipient's name or department)
·From: (Sender's name or department)
·Date: (Date when the memo is written)
·Subject: (Brief description of the memo's purpose)

2. **Introduction**: The introduction briefly states the reason for writing the memo. It provides context and sets the tone for the rest of the message.

3. **Body**: The body of the memo elaborates on the main message. This section can include details, explanations, instructions, or any relevant information related to the subject of the memo. Bulleted lists or numbered points may be used for clarity.

4. **Conclusion** or **Call to Action**: The memo usually ends with a conclusion summarizing the main points or a call to action if there are specific tasks or actions required from the recipients.

5. **Closing**: A polite closing is often included at the end of the memo, such as Sincerely or Best regards, followed by the sender's name and job title.

**Example:**

Date: November 24, 2024
To: Marketing Team
From: Emily White, Marketing Manager
Subject: Reminder: Strategy Planning Meeting on November 26, 2024

Dear Team,
   This is a reminder of our upcoming Marketing Strategy Planning Meeting on November 26, 2024, at 10:00 AM in the main conference room.

**Agenda:**
- Review of Q4 marketing performance
- Discussion of upcoming product launch campaigns
- Budget allocation for Q1 2025

Please ensure to bring your department's report and any suggestions for improvement to the meeting.

Best regards,
Emily White
Marketing Manager


**Meeting Reminder Memo**

Date: [MM/DD/YYYY]
To: [Recipient Name(s) or Department(s)]
From: [Your Name]
Subject: Reminder: [Meeting Title] on [Date and Time]

Purpose:
This memo serves as a reminder for the upcoming meeting.

**Meeting Details:**
- Date: [Meeting Date]
- Time: [Meeting Time]
- Location: [Meeting Location]
- Agenda: [Brief overview of the meeting agenda]

**Preparation Needed:**
Please come prepared with [specific documents, reports, etc.]

# Email Writing

Email writing is a fundamental form of communication used for personal, academic, and professional purposes. A well-crafted email is concise, clear, and courteous, ensuring the message is effectively delivered and understood by the recipient.

**Key Components of an Email:**
1. Subject Line:
2. A short, specific line summarizing the email's purpose. Example: "Request for Meeting Agenda – March 2024".
3. Greeting/Salutation:
4. Begin with a polite greeting based on the relationship with the recipient.
    - Formal: "Dear [Name],"
    - Informal: "Hi [Name],"
5. Opening Line:
6. Start with a friendly or relevant remark. Example: "I hope this email finds you well."
7. Body:
    - Clearly state the purpose of the email.
    - Keep paragraphs short and focused.
    - Use bullet points for clarity if listing multiple items.
8. Closing Line:
9. Politely summarize or provide next steps. Example: "I look forward to your response."
10. Sign-Off:
    - Formal: "Sincerely," or "Best regards,"
    - Informal: "Best," or "Cheers,"
11. Signature:
12. Include your full name, title, and contact details for professional emails.

## Tips for Effective Email Writing:

- Be Clear and Concise: Avoid lengthy introductions or irrelevant details.
- Maintain Professionalism: Use polite and formal language for work-related emails.
- Proofread: Check for grammar, spelling, and tone errors before sending.
- Use Formatting Sparingly: Bold or italicize only key points to enhance readability.
- Respond Promptly: Reply to emails within a reasonable timeframe (24–48 hours, if possible).

## Common Email Types:

1. Formal Email: Used for job applications, business communication, or academic purposes.
2. Informal Email: Casual tone, typically for friends or family.
3. Follow-Up Email: Sent to remind or confirm after a previous conversation or meeting.
4. Marketing Email: Used by businesses to promote products or services.

To: myeslprof@gmai.com

Subject: Query Regarding Online Classes Timings and Duration

Dear [Recipient's Name],

I hope this email finds you well. I am writing to inquire about the schedule and duration of the online classes offered by you.

Please let me know if there are any prerequisites or additional information I should consider. I look forward to your response.

Thank you for your assistance!

Best regards,
[Your Full Name]
[Your Contact Information]

# Pronunciation Guide

Here's a breakdown of vowel sounds in terms of their place of articulation and manner:

1. **Monophthongs**:
- **High Front Vowels:**
- /i/: High front, close vowel. Tongue is close to the roof of the mouth and pushed forward.
- /ɪ/: High front, near-close vowel. Tongue is slightly lower and less tense than /i/.
- **High Back Vowels:**
- /u/: High back, close vowel. Tongue is close to the roof of the mouth and pushed backward.
- /ʊ/: High back, near-close vowel. Tongue is slightly lower and less tense than /u/.
- **Mid Front Vowels:**
- /e/: Mid front, close-mid vowel. Tongue is raised towards the roof of the mouth and pushed forward.
- /ɛ/: Mid front, open-mid vowel. Tongue is lowered and slightly retracted compared to /e/.
- **Mid Back Vowels:**
- /o/: Mid back, close-mid vowel. Tongue is raised towards the roof of the mouth and pushed backward.
- /ɔ/: Mid back, open-mid vowel. Tongue is lowered and slightly retracted compared to /o/.
- **Low Front Vowels:**
- /æ/: Low front, open vowel. Tongue is low and spread out in the mouth.
- **Low Back Vowels:**
- /ɑ/: Low back, open vowel. Tongue is low and pushed backward.

2. **Diphthongs**:
- **Closing Diphthongs:**
- /eɪ/: Starts as /e/ and moves towards /ɪ/.
- /aɪ/: Starts as /a/ and moves towards /ɪ/.
- /ɔɪ/: Starts as /ɔ/ and moves towards /ɪ/.
- /aʊ/: Starts as /a/ and moves towards /ʊ/.
- /oʊ/: Starts as /o/ and moves towards /ʊ/.
- **Centering Diphthongs:**
- /ɪə/: Starts as /ɪ/ and moves towards /ə/.
- /eɔ/: Starts as /e/ and moves towards /ə/.
- /ʊə/: Starts as /ʊ/ and moves towards /ə/.

Consonants are classified based on various articulatory features such as place of articulation, manner of articulation, and voicing. Here's a breakdown of the types of consonants:

1. **Voiced** and **Voiceless**: Consonants can be voiced or voiceless depending on whether the vocal cords vibrate during their production. For example, 'b' is voiced (/b/), while 'p' is voiceless (/p/).

2. **Manner of Articulation:**
   - **Stops** (or **plosives**): Consonants produced by completely obstructing the airflow and then releasing it. Examples: /p/, /b/, /t/, /d/, /k/, /g/.
   - **Fricatives**: Consonants produced by narrowing the airflow through a small passage, creating friction. Examples: /f/, /v/, /s/, /z/, /ʃ/, /ʒ/.
   - **Affricates**: Consonants that begin as stops and release into fricatives. Examples: /tʃ/ (as in church), /dʒ/ (as in judge).
   - **Nasals**: Consonants produced by directing airflow through the nasal cavity. Examples: /m/, /n/, /ŋ/ (as in sing).
   - **Approximants**: Consonants produced by creating a narrowing but not a complete closure in the vocal tract. Examples: /w/, /j/ (as in yes).
   - **Lateral approximants**: Consonants produced with airflow along the sides of the tongue. Example: /l/.

3. **Place** of **Articulation**: This refers to where in the vocal tract the obstruction of airflow occurs.
   - **Bilabial**: Consonants produced using both lips. Examples: /p/, /b/.
   - **Labiodental**: Consonants produced with the lower lip against the upper teeth. Examples: /f/, /v/.
   - **Dental**: Consonants produced with the tongue against the teeth. Examples: /θ/ (as in think), /ð/ (as in this).
   - **Alveolar**: Consonants produced with the tongue against or near the alveolar ridge. Examples: /t/, /d/, /s/, /z/.
   - **Palatal**: Consonants produced with the middle part of the tongue against the hard palate. Examples: /ʃ/ (as in ship), /ʒ/ (as in measure).
   - **Velar**: Consonants produced with the back of the tongue against the soft palate (velum). Examples: /k/, /g/.
   - **Glottal**: Consonants produced with the closure or narrowing of the glottis. Example: /h/.

4. **Other Classifications:**
   - **Sonorants**: Consonants produced with relatively free airflow. Includes nasals, approximants, and some fricatives.
   - **Obstruents**: Consonants produced with a significant obstruction of airflow. Includes stops, fricatives, and affricates

# Digraphs

A digraph is a combination of two letters that represent a single sound. In English, digraphs are commonly used to represent sounds that cannot be easily represented by a single letter. Here are some common digraphs in English:

1. **Consonant Digraphs:**
   - ch (/tʃ/ sound as in church)
   - sh (/ʃ/ sound as in shoe)
   - th (/θ/ sound as in think or /ð/ sound as in this)
   - ph (/f/ sound as in phone)
   - wh (/ʍ/ or /w/ sound as in what)

2. **Vowel Digraphs:**
   - ai (/eɪ/ sound as in rain)
   - ay (/eɪ/ sound as in day )
   - ee (/iː/ sound as in bee )
   - ea (various sounds, such as /iː/ in sea or /ɛ/ in bread)
   - oa (/oʊ/ sound as in boat)
   - oo (various sounds, such as /uː/ in moon or /ʊ/ in book)

3. **Silent Digraphs:**
   - gh (often silent, as in light or night)
   - kn (the k is silent, as in knee )
   - wr (the w is silent, as in write )

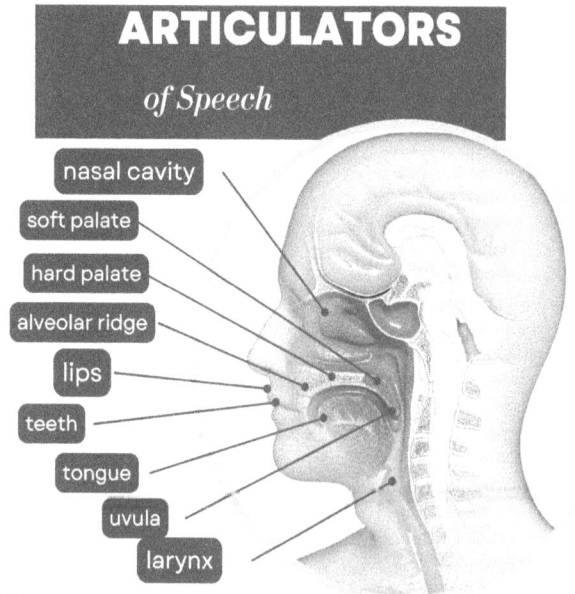

# IPA Pronunciation Chart
## Consonants

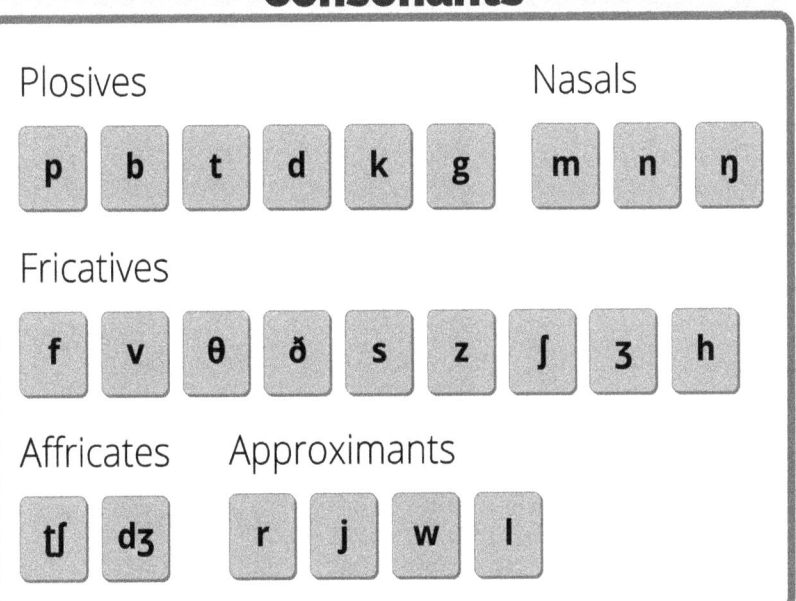

## Vowels

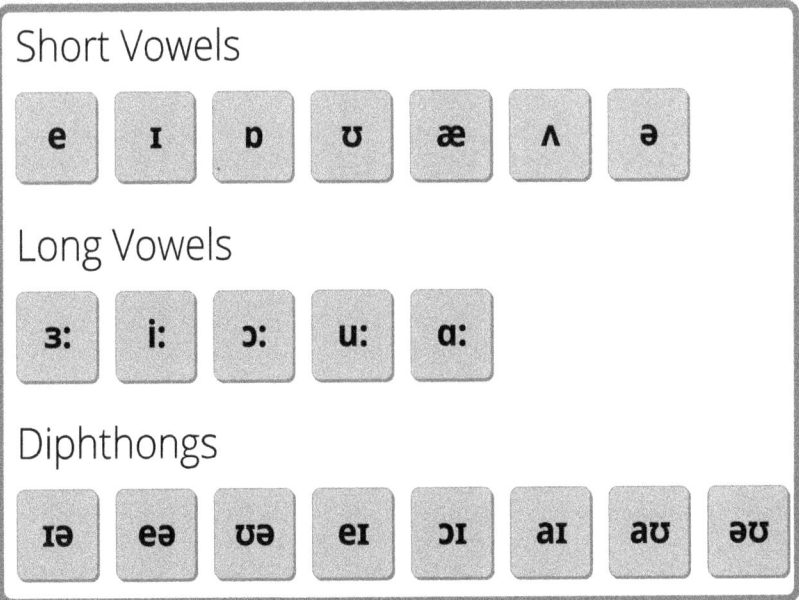

Certainly! Below are the 44 sounds of the English alphabet pronounced in initial, medial, and final positions, represented using the International Phonetic Alphabet (IPA) symbols:

# Consonant Sounds

| Initial Position | Medial Position | Final Position |
|---|---|---|
| **1.Stops:** | **1.Stops:** | **1.Stops:** |
| ·/p/: "pat" | ·/p/: "happy" | ·/p/: "cup" |
| ·/b/: "bat" | ·/b/: "rabbit" | ·/b/: "rib" |
| ·/t/: "top" | ·/t/: "better" | ·/t/: "cat" |
| ·/d/: "dog" | ·/d/: "ladder" | ·/d/: "bed" |
| ·/k/: "cat" | ·/k/: "monkey" | ·/k/: "back" |
| ·/g/: "go" | ·/g/: "bigger" | ·/g/: "bag" |
| **2.Fricatives:** | **2.Fricatives:** | **2.Fricatives:** |
| ·/f/: "fan" | ·/f/: "coffee" | ·/f/: "leaf" |
| ·/v/: "van" | ·/v/: "driving" | ·/v/: "love" |
| ·/θ/: "thin" | ·/θ/: "author" | ·/θ/: "bath" |
| ·/ð/: "this" | ·/ð/: "weather" | ·/ð/: "bathe" |
| ·/s/: "sun" | ·/s/: "dessert" | ·/s/: "bus" |
| ·/z/: "zip" | ·/z/: "losing" | ·/z/: "nose" |
| ·/ʃ/: "shoe" | ·/ʃ/: "machine" | ·/ʃ/: "dish" |
| ·/ʒ/: "measure" | ·/ʒ/: "pleasure" | ·/ʒ/: "garage" |
| **3.Affricates:** | **3.Affricates:** | **3.Affricates:** |
| ·/tʃ/: "church" | ·/tʃ/: "picture" | ·/tʃ/: "watch" |
| ·/dʒ/: "judge" | ·/dʒ/: "soldier" | ·/dʒ/: "badge" |
| **4.Nasals:** | **4.Nasals:** | **4.Nasals:** |
| ·/m/: "man" | ·/m/: "summer" | ·/m/: "gum" |
| ·/n/: "no" | ·/n/: "button" | ·/n/: "run" |
| ·/ŋ/: "sing" | ·/ŋ/: "singer" | ·/ŋ/: "song" |
| **5.Approximants:** | **5.Approximants:** | **5.Approximants:** |
| ·/l/: "leg" | ·/l/: "table" | ·/l/: "apple" |
| ·/r/: "run" | ·/r/: "carrot" | ·/r/: "star" |
| ·/w/: "wet" | ·/w/: "window" | ·/w/: "cow" |
| ·/j/: "yes" | ·/j/: "canyon" | ·/j/: "toy" |
| **6.Others:** | | |
| ·/h/: "hat" | | |

Top of Form

# Vowel Sounds

## Initial Position

**Monophthongs:**
1. /i/ (as in "eat")
2. /e/ (as in "egg")
3. /ɛ/ (as in "end")
4. /æ/ (as in "apple")
5. /ɑ/ (as in "art")
6. /ɔ/ (as in "on")
7. /ʊ/ (as in "up")
8. /u/ (as in "use")
9. /ə/ (as in "about")
10. /ɪ/ (as in "it")

**Diphthongs:**
11. /eɪ/ (as in "ape")
12. /aɪ/ (as in "ice")
13. /ɔɪ/ (as in "oil")
14. /aʊ/ (as in "out")
15. /oʊ/ (as in "old")
16. /ɪə/ (as in "ear")
17. /eə/ (as in "air")
18. /ʊə/ (as in "tour")
19. /aɪə/ (as in "hire")
20. /aʊə/ (as in "hour")

## Medial Position

**Monophthongs:**
1. /ɪ/ - As in "sit"
2. /e/ - As in "bet"
3. /æ/ - As in "cat"
4. /ɑː/ - As in "car"
5. /ɔː/ - As in "dog"
6. /ʊ/ - As in "book"
7. /ə/ - As in "sofa"
8. /iː/ - As in "seat"
9. /ɛ/ - As in "set"
10. /ʌ/ - As in "cut"
11. /ɜː/ - As in "fern"
12. /ɒ/ - As in "hot"
13. /uː/ - As in "boot"

**Diphthongs:**
1. /eɪ/ - As in "say"
2. /aɪ/ - As in "time"
3. /ɔɪ/ - As in "boy"
4. /aʊ/ - As in "cow"
5. /ɪə/ - As in "beer"
6. /eə/ - As in "care"
7. /ʊə/ - As in "pure"
8. /əʊ/ - As in "goat"

## Final Position

**Monophthongs:**
1. "Feet" - /iː/ (as in "feet")
2. "Cat" - /æ/ (as in "cat")
3. "Dog" - /ɒ/ (as in "dog")
4. "Fog" - /ɔː/ (as in "fog")
5. "Goose" - /uː/ (as in "goose")
6. "Bit" - /ɪ/ (as in "bit")
7. "Caught" - /ɔː/ (as in "caught")
8. "Far" - /ɑː/ (as in "far")
9. "Dot" - /ɒ/ (as in "dot")
10. "Wit" - /ɪ/ (as in "wit")

**Diphthongs:**
11. "Boy" - /ɔɪ/ (as in "boy")
12. "Toy" - /ɔɪ/ (as in "toy")
13. "Lie" - /aɪ/ (as in "lie")
14. "Eye" - /aɪ/ (as in "eye")
15. "Cow" - /aʊ/ (as in "cow")
16. "Now" - /aʊ/ (as in "now")
17. "Hear" - /ɪə/ (as in "hear")
18. "Near" - /ɪə/ (as in "near")
19. "Boat" - /əʊ/ (as in "boat")
20. "Flow" - /əʊ/ (as in "flow")

# BASIC VOCABULARY

Here's a list of daily conversations for school categorized into various school-related situations. These conversations are tailored for students, teachers, and school activities, making them practical and engaging.

## 1. Classroom Conversations

1. Greeting the Teacher
   - Student: Good morning, Ma'am/Sir!
   - Teacher: Good morning! How are you today?
2. Asking a Question
   - Student: Excuse me, can you explain this again?
   - Teacher: Sure, let me go over it one more time.
3. Borrowing a Pencil
   - Student A: Can I borrow a pencil?
   - Student B: Sure, here you go.
4. Talking About Homework
   - Student A: Did you finish your homework?
   - Student B: Not yet, I'll complete it during lunch.
5. Asking for Help
   - Student: I don't understand this question.
   - Teacher: Let's solve it together.

## 2. Conversations During Break Time

1. Choosing Games to Play
   - Student A: What game should we play today?
   - Student B: Let's play hide-and-seek!
2. Sharing Snacks
   - Student A: Would you like some chips?
   - Student B: Yes, thank you!
3. Talking About Weekend Plans
   - Student A: What are you doing this weekend?
   - Student B: I'm going to visit my grandparents.
4. Discussing Favorite Subjects
   - Student A: What's your favorite subject?
   - Student B: I love math. What about you?
5. Making New Friends
- Student A: Hi, can I join you?
- Student B: Of course! Come sit with us.

## 3. Teacher-Student Conversations

1. Submitting Homework
   - Student: Here's my homework, Sir/Ma'am.
   - Teacher: Thank you. Let me check it later.
2. Asking for Permission
   - Student: May I go to the restroom?
   - Teacher: Yes, but be quick.
3. Answering Questions
   - Teacher: Who can solve this problem?
   - Student: I can, Ma'am!
4. Getting Feedback
   - Student: How did I do on the test?
   - Teacher: You did well, but you need to improve your spelling.
5. Explaining Rules
   - Teacher: No talking during the test.
   - Student: Understood, Ma'am.

## 4. Group Work and Projects

1. Assigning Roles
   - Student A: Who wants to do the introduction?
   - Student B: I'll do it!
2. Discussing Ideas
   - Student A: What should we include in our project?
   - Student B: Let's add some images and a chart.
3. Asking for Clarifications
   - Student: What's our deadline for this project?
   - Teacher: It's due next Friday.
4. Helping a Friend
   - Student A: Can you help me with this section?
   - Student B: Sure, let's work on it together.
5. Presenting a Project
   - Student A: Let's rehearse our presentation.
   - Student B: Good idea. I'll start with my part.

## 5. Conversations in the School Library

1. Borrowing a Book
   - Student: Can I borrow this book, please?
   - Librarian: Sure, return it by next Monday.
2. Finding a Book
   - Student: Where can I find history books?
   - Librarian: They're on the second shelf to the left.
3. Requesting Silence
   - Librarian: Please keep your voices down.
   - Student: Sorry, we'll be quiet.
4. Returning a Book
   - Student: I'd like to return this book.
   - Librarian: Thank you. Did you enjoy it?
5. Asking About Overdue Fines
   - Student: Do I have to pay a fine for returning this late?
   - Librarian: Yes, it's $1 per day.

## 6. Sports and Physical Education

1. Choosing Teams
   - Student A: Who wants to be on my team?
   - Student B: I'll join!
2. Asking About the Game
   - Student: What game are we playing today?
   - Coach: We're playing basketball.
3. Encouraging Teammates
   - Student A: Come on, we can win this!
   - Student B: Yes, let's do our best!
4. Requesting Equipment
   - Student: Can I borrow a football?
   - PE Teacher: Sure, just return it after practice.
5. Cheering for Friends
   - Student A: Great goal!
   - Student B: Thanks!

## 7. Conversations About Tests and Exams
1. Discussing the Exam Schedule
   - Student A: When is the math exam?
   - Student B: It's on Friday.
2. Asking About Exam Format
   - Student: Will the test be multiple choice?
   - Teacher: Yes, but there will also be essay questions.
3. Talking About Preparation
   - Student A: How are you preparing for the exam?
   - Student B: I'm revising my notes.
4. After the Exam
   - Student A: How was the test?
   - Student B: It was tricky, but I think I did okay.
5. Getting Results
   - Student: Did we get the results for the test?
   - Teacher: I'll give them to you tomorrow.

## 8. Conversations in the School Bus
1. Finding a Seat
   - Student A: Is this seat taken?
   - Student B: No, you can sit here.
2. Talking About the Route
   - Student A: How long does it take to get home?
   - Student B: About 20 minutes.
3. Sharing Snacks
   - Student A: Do you want some cookies?
   - Student B: Yes, please!
4. Discussing School Events
   - Student A: Are you going to the sports day?
   - Student B: Yes, I'm in the relay race.
5. Making Plans for Tomorrow
   - Student A: Let's study together after school tomorrow.
   - Student B: Sure, that sounds good.

## 9. Conversations with Friends

1. Planning a Group Study
   - Student A: When should we meet for the project?
   - Student B: Let's meet after school on Wednesday.
2. Talking About Hobbies
   - Student A: What's your favorite hobby?
   - Student B: I love painting. What about you?
3. Discussing a School Trip
   - Student A: Are you excited about the trip?
   - Student B: Yes, I can't wait!
4. Helping a Friend
   - Student A: I forgot my lunch today.
   - Student B: Here, you can share mine.
5. Talking About New Teachers
   - Student A: What do you think of the new math teacher?
   - Student B: She's very kind and explains well.

## 10. Parent-Teacher Meetings

1. Greeting the Teacher
   - Parent: Good morning, how is my child doing?
   - Teacher: Good morning! Your child is doing very well.
2. Asking About Progress
   - Parent: How are his grades?
   - Teacher: He's improving a lot in science.
3. Discussing Weak Areas
   - Parent: What subjects need more attention?
   - Teacher: Math could use some extra practice.
4. Feedback for the Parent
   - Teacher: Please encourage reading at home.
   - Parent: Sure, I'll make sure of that.
5. Thanking the Teacher
   - Parent: Thank you for your guidance.
   - Teacher: You're welcome.

# Adjectives and Opposites

- Active - Inactive
- Adept - Inept
- Adorable - Unattractive
- Aggressive - Passive
- Agreeable - Disagreeable
- Alone - Accompanied
- Ancient - Modern
- Angry - Calm
- Artistic - Unartistic
- Attractive - Unattractive
- Amazed - Unimpressed
- Abundant - Scarce
- Authentic - Fake
- Arrogant - Humble
- Average - Exceptional
- Alert - Drowsy
- Absent - Present
- Accurate - Inaccurate
- Ample - Insufficient
- Artificial - Natural
- Aged - Young
- Attentive - Neglectful
- Ascetic - Indulgent
- Astonishing - Unremarkable
- Aggressive - Gentle
- Angelic - Devilish
- Anxious - Relaxed
- Assured - Uncertain
- Abundant - Scarcity
- Avid - Indifferent
- Amusing - Boring
- Awful - Wonderful
- Astute - Naive
- Authentic - Counterfeit
- Arid - Moist
- Brave - Cowardly
- Bright - Dim
- Bold - Timid
- Big - Small
- Bitter - Sweet

- Blunt - Sharp
- Boring - Exciting
- Benevolent - Malevolent
- Beautiful - Ugly
- Blurry - Clear
- Busy - Idle
- Brilliant - Dull
- Bumpy - Smooth
- Brisk - Lethargic
- Bright-eyed - Bleary-eyed
- Balanced - Unbalanced
- Big-hearted - Cold-hearted
- Brash - Polite
- Bulky - Slim
- Beneficial - Harmful
- Basic - Complex
- Blazing - Cool
- Benevolent - Malevolent
- Blunt - Sharp
- Blissful - Miserable
- Brutal - Gentle
- Boundless - Limited
- Bright - Dark
- Brisk - Slow
- Boring - Interesting
- Bitter - Sweet
- Brash - Reserved
- Buoyant - Heavy
- Bold - Shy
- Bizarre - Ordinary
- Calm - Agitated
- Cold - Hot
- Clean - Dirty
- Clear - Cloudy
- Cheap - Expensive
- Cautious - Reckless
- Cruel - Kind
- Clever - Dull
- Confident - Shy
- Comfortable - Uncomfortable

- Crisp - Soggy
- Curious - Indifferent
- Capable - Incapable
- Complete - Incomplete
- Crowded - Empty
- Cool - Warm
- Colorful - Dull
- Careful - Careless
- Charming - Unpleasant
- Complex - Simple
- Casual - Formal
- Cheerful - Gloomy
- Contemporary - Traditional
- Confusing - Clear
- Courageous - Timid
- Clumsy - Graceful
- Consistent - Inconsistent
- Creative - Unimaginative
- Crucial - Trivial
- Cautious - Careless
- Calm - Tense
- Charismatic - Uncharismatic
- Clean - Messy
- Carefree - Worried
- Compact - Spacious
- Dark - Light
- Delicate - Durable
- Deep - Shallow
- Dry - Wet
- Dull - Sharp
- Dynamic - Static
- Distant - Near
- Dirty - Clean
- Discreet - Indiscreet
- Dense - Sparse
- Daring - Timid
- Delightful - Unpleasant
- Disorganized - Organized
- Dramatic - Unremarkable
- Difficult - Easy
- Dreamy - Realistic
- Detached - Attached
- Down-to-earth - Idealistic
- Democratic - Autocratic
- Deceptive - Honest
- Dull - Exciting
- Dignified - Undignified
- Definite - Vague
- Dynamic - Monotonous
- Delicious - Disgusting
- Divine - Earthly
- Direct - Indirect
- Discreet - Blatant
- Determined - Indecisive
- Diminutive - Gargantuan
- Decisive - Indecisive
- Dramatic - Calm
- Doubtful - Certain
- Desolate - Populated
- Distinct - Indistinct
- Easy - Difficult
- Early - Late
- Energetic - Lethargic
- Exciting - Boring
- Elegant - Unrefined
- Exotic - Common
- Exact - Approximate
- Efficient - Inefficient
- Eccentric - Conventional
- Enthusiastic - Apathetic
- Exclusive - Inclusive
- Expensive - Cheap
- Endless - Finite
- Emotional - Unemotional

- Evil - Good
- Eloquent - Inarticulate
- Extraordinary - Ordinary
- Enormous - Tiny
- Evident - Unclear
- Energetic - Tired
- Exuberant - Subdued
- Easygoing - Stressed
- Ebullient - Reserved
- Elegant - Clumsy
- Everlasting - Temporary
- Excited - Calm
- Enthusiastic - Disinterested
- Evasive - Direct
- Enduring - Fragile
- Emphatic - Unemphatic
- Expansive - Restrictive
- Effervescent - Flat
- Enlightened - Ignorant
- Eager - Apathetic
- Established - New
- Friendly - Hostile
- Fast - Slow
- Fresh - Stale
- Fierce - Gentle
- Full - Empty
- Flexible - Rigid
- Famous - Unknown
- Frightening - Calm
- Fat - Thin
- Faithful - Unfaithful
- Free - Restricted
- Funky - Plain
- Faded - Vivid
- Funny - Serious
- Fragrant - Odorless
- Firm - Soft
- Feeble - Strong
- Favorable - Unfavorable
- Furry - Smooth
- Fuzzy - Clear
- Flimsy - Sturdy
- Fashionable - Unfashionable
- Formal - Casual
- Flammable - Non-flammable
- Fragile - Durable
- Foolish - Wise
- Full-bodied - Diluted
- Fertile - Barren
- Frosty - Warm
- Faulty - Flawless
- Fastidious - Careless
- Faint - Strong
- Feisty - Submissive
- Familiar - Unfamiliar
- Functional - Nonfunctional
- Gentle - Harsh
- Good - Bad
- Grand - Modest
- Genuine - Fake
- Greedy - Generous
- Glowing - Dull
- Grim - Cheerful
- Green - Mature
- Gregarious - Introverted
- Great - Terrible
- Gloomy - Bright
- Gargantuan - Tiny
- Gallant - Cowardly
- Gracious - Rude
- Gritty - Smooth
- Giddy - Serious
- Glaring - Subtle
- Glum - Jovial

- Gold - Silver (if referring to color or quality)
- Glistening - Dull
- Glorious - Unremarkable
- Grimy - Clean
- Glacial - Tropical
- Generous - Selfish
- Gross - Refined
- Grown-up - Childish
- Genuine - Phony
- Gargantuan - Minuscule
- Grateful - Ungrateful
- Gloomy - Sunny
- Galloping - Stationary
- Gutsy - Timid
- Hard - Soft
- High - Low
- Healthy - Unhealthy
- Honest - Dishonest
- Heavy - Light
- Hot - Cool
- Humble - Arrogant
- Harsh - Gentle
- Hasty - Slow
- Helpful - Unhelpful
- Hollow - Solid
- Hearty - Weak
- Horrific - Pleasant
- Historical - Modern
- Horrible - Wonderful
- Happy - Sad
- Hot - Cold
- High-pitched - Low-pitched
- Hesitant - Confident
- Harmonious - Discordant
- Hardworking - Lazy
- Hypocritical - Genuine
- Interesting - Boring
- Intelligent - Unintelligent
- Irritated - Calm
- Immense - Tiny
- Innovative - Unoriginal
- Important - Trivial
- Innocent - Guilty
- Inclusive - Exclusive
- Industrious - Lazy
- Incredible - Ordinary
- Impatient - Patient
- Intimate - Distant
- Impressive - Unimpressive
- Ideal - Imperfect
- Icy - Warm
- Intellectual - Nonintellectual
- Insecure - Confident
- Idle - Active
- Inconsistent - Consistent
- Incredible - Believable
- Insubordinate - Obedient
- Inaccessible - Accessible
- Insensitive - Sensitive
- Invisible - Visible
- Irregular - Regular
- Imposing - Unimposing
- Indifferent - Concerned
- Immortal - Mortal
- Insufficient - Sufficient
- Irrational - Rational
- Illogical - Logical
- Intuitive - Unintuitive
- Insincere - Sincere
- Immediate - Delayed
- Joyful - Sad
- Jovial - Serious
- Jumpy - Calm
- Just - Unjust
- Jaded - Fresh
- Jazzy - Plain

- Jolly - Miserable
- Jealous - Content
- Jumpy - Stable
- Jumbled - Organized
- Jubilant - Disheartened
- Jaded - Eager
- Judicious - Foolish
- Juicy - Dry
- Jovial - Grumpy
- Jazzy - Dull
- Jumpy - Relaxed
- Jaded - Excited
- Jarring - Soothing
- Joyous - Gloomy
- Jovial - Sullen
- Jumbled - Ordered
- Jumpy - Composed
- Justified - Unjustified
- Jovial - Somber
- Jaded - Optimistic
- Jubilant - Despondent
- Jolly - Downcast
- Jeering - Supportive
- Jumpy - Steady
- Jeer - Praise
- Jaded - New
- Jovial - Melancholic
- Jubilant - Depressed
- Jealous - Unconcerned
- Kind - Cruel
- Keen - Apathetic
- Knowledgeable - Ignorant
- Keen-eyed - Blind
- Kooky - Serious
- Kempt - Unkempt
- Keen - Dull
- Knotty - Smooth
- Keen - Indifferent

- Kaleidoscopic - Monochrome
- Kingly - Common
- Knockout - Unremarkable
- Keen - Lethargic
- Knobby - Flat
- Known - Unknown
- Keen - Dull
- Keen-witted - Slow-witted
- Keen - Blunt
- Karmic - Non-karmic
- Kid-friendly - Adult-oriented
- Kinetic - Static
- Keen - Apathetic
- Keen-sighted - Myopic
- Kosher - Unfit
- Kaleidoscopic - Uniform
- Kicky - Dull
- Keen - Indifferent
- Knowledgeable - Uninformed
- Keen - Uninterested
- Kooky - Conventional
- Knotty - Straightforward
- Keen - Dull
- Kind - Unkind
- Keen - Apathetic
- Keen-edged - Dull-edged
- Lively - Lethargic
- Loud - Quiet
- Long - Short
- Light - Heavy
- Lazy - Energetic
- Lovely - Unpleasant
- Low - High
- Luminous - Dim
- Logical - Illogical
- Lush - Sparse
- Loose - Tight

- Lackluster - Brilliant
- Lively - Dull
- Loyal - Disloyal
- Large - Small
- Luminous - Dark
- Lively - Boring
- Luxurious - Basic
- Limp - Firm
- Lurid - Subdued
- Lively - Dead
- Luminous - Opaque
- Legitimate - Illegitimate
- Larger - Smaller
- Lyrical - Prosaic
- Light-hearted - Serious
- Lean - Fat
- Languid - Vigorous
- Lethargic - Alert
- Low-key - Flashy
- Lively - Dull
- Lively - Flat
- Lackadaisical - Diligent
- Linear - Nonlinear
- Literate - Illiterate
- Mild - Intense
- Modern - Old-fashioned
- Mighty - Weak
- Mysterious - Obvious
- Mature - Immature
- Massive - Tiny
- Moist - Dry
- Melancholic - Joyful
- Mundane - Exciting
- Mellow - Harsh
- Mild - Intense
- Modern - Old-fashioned
- Mighty - Weak
- Mysterious - Obvious
- Mature - Immature
- Massive - Tiny
- Moist - Dry
- Melancholic - Joyful
- Mundane - Exciting
- Mellow - Harsh
- Magnificent - Unimpressive
- Mellow - Harsh
- Mean - Kind
- Mediocre - Excellent
- Mournful - Cheerful
- Massive - Minor
- Mature - Juvenile
- Mythical - Real
- Monotonous - Varied
- Macho - Gentle
- Mystical - Literal
- Motivated - Unmotivated
- Magical - Ordinary
- Methodical - Chaotic
- Minimal - Excessive
- Mellow - Harsh
- Mysterious - Clear
- Mediocre - Outstanding
- Mighty - Feeble
- Masculine - Feminine
- Mature - Naive
- Messy - Neat
- Mellow - Intense
- Mild - Extreme
- Meager - Abundant
- Nervous - Calm
- Noble - Base
- New - Old
- Noisy - Quiet
- Natural - Artificial
- Narrow - Wide
- Neat - Messy

- Normal - Abnormal
- Numb - Sensitive
- Nightly - Daily
- Nasty - Pleasant
- Necessary - Unnecessary
- Nourishing - Depleting
- Nurturing - Neglectful
- Noble - Dishonorable
- Nurtured - Neglected
- Naked - Clothed
- Negative - Positive
- Noble - Common
- Neat - Sloppy
- Numb - Responsive
- Nimble - Slow
- Nonchalant - Anxious
- Nostalgic - Indifferent
- Notable - Unremarkable
- Numerous - Few
- Nutritious - Unhealthy
- Narrow - Expansive
- Natural - Synthetic
- Noble - Vulgar
- Nasty - Nice
- New - Used
- Neutral - Partisan
- Needy - Self-sufficient
- Old - New
- Open - Closed
- Ordinary - Extraordinary
- Obvious - Subtle
- Optimistic - Pessimistic
- Opaque - Transparent
- Organic - Synthetic
- Overweight - Underweight
- Orderly - Chaotic
- Outstanding - Mediocre
- Ominous - Promising

- Obedient - Disobedient
- Occasional - Frequent
- Offensive - Inoffensive
- Old-fashioned - Modern
- Overwhelming - Underwhelming
- Open-minded - Closed-minded
- Original - Copycat
- Optimistic - Cynical
- Obscure - Clear
- Outdated - Up-to-date
- Obtrusive - Discreet
- Opulent - Modest
- Obvious - Hidden
- Overconfident - Underconfident
- Organized - Disorganized
- Ominous - Cheerful
- Outgoing - Introverted
- Ordinary - Exceptional
- Obligatory - Optional
- Open - Restrictive
- Overjoyed - Disappointed
- On-time - Late
- Obedient - Rebellious
- Overflowing - Empty
- Polite - Rude
- Powerful - Weak
- Punctual - Late
- Proud - Ashamed
- Positive - Negative
- Practical - Impractical
- Plain - Fancy
- Precise - Vague
- Patient - Impatient
- Passive - Active
- Public - Private
- Perfect - Imperfect
- Particular - General
- Pale - Dark

- Predictable - Unpredictable
- Persistent - Fleeting
- Peaceful - Aggressive
- Pale - Vivid
- Pernicious - Beneficial
- Powerful - Ineffectual
- Pretentious - Modest
- Pungent - Mild
- Pessimistic - Optimistic
- Proficient - Inept
- Prolific - Unproductive
- Pleasant - Unpleasant
- Peculiar - Normal
- Plentiful - Scarce
- Precious - Valueless
- Pliant - Rigid
- Plausible - Implausible
- Pale - Bright
- Persistent - Temporary
- Pale - Colorful
- Pristine - Dirty
- Quiet - Loud
- Quick - Slow
- Quality - Inferior
- Quaint - Modern
- Qualified - Unqualified
- Quizzical - Serious
- Quenching - Thirsty
- Quotable - Unremarkable
- Quiescent - Active
- Quirky - Conventional
- Quintessential - Unessential
- Quizzical - Straightforward
- Quasi - Absolute
- Quiet - Noisy
- Quick-witted - Slow-witted
- Quaint - Ordinary
- Qualified - Unskilled
- Quotidian - Extraordinary
- Quintuple - Single
- Quality - Substandard
- Quarrelsome - Peaceful
- Radiant - Dull
- Rough - Smooth
- Reliable - Unreliable
- Rich - Poor
- Rigid - Flexible
- Rapid - Slow
- Rude - Polite
- Reckless - Cautious
- Rustic - Urban
- Remarkable - Unremarkable
- Rebellious - Compliant
- Reluctant - Eager
- Rational - Irrational
- Robust - Fragile
- Respectful - Disrespectful
- Reserved - Outgoing
- Ravenous - Full
- Regular - Irregular
- Rancid - Fresh
- Resilient - Weak
- Radiant - Dim
- Repetitive - Varied
- Reputable - Disreputable
- Recessive - Dominant
- Ruthless - Compassionate
- Rigorous - Lenient
- Roaring - Quiet
- Rusty - Polished
- Romantic - Unromantic
- Rough - Fine
- Resplendent - Dull
- Robust - Fragile
- Revolutionary - Traditional
- Reclusive - Sociable

- Soft - Hard
- Silent - Noisy
- Simple - Complex
- Secure - Insecure
- Sharp - Dull
- Sweet - Bitter
- Small - Large
- Sincere - Insincere
- Stable - Unstable
- Subtle - Obvious
- Sunny - Cloudy
- Safe - Dangerous
- Slow - Fast
- Stubborn - Flexible
- Serene - Agitated
- Strange - Familiar
- Sane - Insane
- Slight - Significant
- Satisfactory - Unsatisfactory
- Sober - Drunk
- Solid - Liquid
- Shy - Outgoing
- Sharp - Blunt
- Smooth - Rough
- Superficial - Deep
- Stingy - Generous
- Strong - Weak
- Squalid - Clean
- Sensitive - Insensitive
- Steady - Wobbly
- Secular - Religious
- Suspicious - Trusting
- Selective - Indiscriminate
- Serious - Light-hearted
- Synchronized - Out of sync
- Tall - Short
- Turbulent - Calm
- Tired - Energetic
- Traditional - Modern
- Timid - Bold
- Thick - Thin
- Trendy - Outdated
- Tense - Relaxed
- Tangible - Intangible
- Transparent - Opaque
- Terrific - Awful
- Trivial - Significant
- Truthful - Dishonest
- Teeming - Empty
- Tame - Wild
- Tasty - Bland
- Turbid - Clear
- Trustworthy - Untrustworthy
- Tactful - Blunt
- Tactile - Abstract
- Thriving - Declining
- Tragic - Comedic
- Tender - Rough
- Tolerant - Intolerant
- Turbulent - Peaceful
- Turbid - Clean
- Tactile - Non-physical
- Temporary - Permanent
- Timely - Delayed
- Teeny - Huge
- Tame - Fierce
- Turbulent - Stable
- Turbid - Clear
- Unusual - Common
- Upbeat - Downbeat
- Uplifted - Depressed
- Unique - Ordinary
- Useless - Useful
- Ultimate - Initial
- Uncertain - Certain

- Useless - Useful
- Ultimate - Initial
- Uncertain - Certain
- Unreliable - Reliable
- Unhappy - Happy
- Unpredictable - Predictable
- Unkempt - Neat
- Uplifting - Demoralizing
- Unfamiliar - Familiar
- Uniform - Varied
- Unbroken - Broken
- Unsettled - Settled
- Unrestricted - Restricted
- Unclear - Clear
- Urgent - Nonurgent
- Uneven - Even
- Untidy - Tidy
- Unusual - Typical
- Underestimated - Overestimated
- Uncertain - Confident
- Unfinished - Finished
- Unyielding - Flexible
- Untouched - Touched
- Unsolved - Solved
- Unworthy - Worthy
- Undisciplined - Disciplined
- Unlikely - Likely
- Unusual - Commonplace
- Undervalued - Valued
- Unadvised - Advised
- Unremarkable - Remarkable
- Vivid - Dull
- Valuable - Worthless
- Vast - Limited
- Vibrant - Lifeless
- Victorious - Defeated
- Vulnerable - Protected
- Vigorous - Weak
- Virtuous - Immoral
- Vacant - Occupied
- Vain - Humble
- Volatile - Stable
- Visible - Invisible
- Vast - Narrow
- Vivid - Faded
- Venerable - Disreputable
- Vivid - Faint
- Voluntary - Involuntary
- Vivid - Muted
- Valid - Invalid
- Vocal - Silent
- Valiant - Cowardly
- Vast - Confined
- Vicious - Kind
- Versatile - Limited
- Voluminous - Compact
- Vibrant - Dull
- Victorious - Submissive
- Venerable - Youthful
- Vocal - Reserved
- Visceral - Rational
- Vivid - Blurry
- Venerable - New
- Vapid - Exciting
- Voluntary - Mandatory
- Warm - Cold
- Wise - Foolish
- Weak - Strong
- Witty - Dull
- Wild - Tame
- Weary - Energetic
- Willing - Unwilling
- Widespread - Localized

- Wet - Dry
- Weak - Powerful
- Well - Ill
- Worldly - Naive
- Wide - Narrow
- Wobbly - Stable
- Wretched - Joyful
- Wholesome - Unwholesome
- Wistful - Content
- Wiry - Soft
- Wise - Ignorant
- Wrinkled - Smooth
- Willing - Reluctant
- Winning - Losing
- Warrior-like - Peaceful
- Weak - Robust
- Whimsical - Serious
- Welcoming - Hostile
- Wondrous - Ordinary
- Watery - Thick
- Wise - Unwise
- Wild - Controlled
- Witty - Dull-witted
- Willing - Uncooperative
- Well-mannered - Rude
- Wary - Trustful
- Wicked - Virtuous
- Young - Old
- Yellow - Blue
- Yummy - Yucky
- Yielding - Stubborn
- Yogic - Non-yogic
- Yarned (related to yarn, cozy) - Plain (uncozy)
- Yonder - Nearby
- Yucky - Tasty
- Yes - No
- Yelling - Whispering
- Yachted (related to yachts, luxurious) - Plain (non-luxurious)
- Yearly - Daily
- Yodeling - Silent
- Yoked - Free
- Young - Aged
- Yielded - Resisted
- Yucky - Delicious
- Yard-long - Short
- Yawn-inducing - Exciting
- Yarn-like - Smooth
- Yogurt-like - Dry
- Yellowish - Bluish
- Yes-man - Independent
- Yam-like - Non-starchy
- Yammering - Silent
- Yummy - Gross
- Youthful - Elderly
- Yankee - Non-American
- Yare (quick and agile) - Slow
- Yearning - Content
- Yucky - Appealing
- Yawn - Alert
- Yielding - Resistant
- Yodel - Mumble
- Yogic - Secular

- Xenophobic - Xenophilic
- Xenial (hospitable) - Hostile
- Xeric (dry) - Hydric (wet)
- X-traordinary (extraordinary) - Ordinary
- Xenogeneic (derived from another species) - Autogenous (derived from the same species)
- Xanadu-like (idyllic) - Dismal
- Xenogenetic (originating from outside) - Endogenous (originating from within)
- Xenon-rich - Xenon-poor
- Xanthic (yellow) - Cyanic (blue)
- Xylophagous (wood-eating) - Non-xylophagous
- Xenolithic (alien or foreign in a geological context) - Indigenous
- Xenocentric (focusing on the outsider's perspective) - Ethnocentric (focusing on one's own group)
- Xylophilous (wood-loving) - Xylophobic (wood-fearing)
- Xanthous (yellowish) - Reddish
- Xenocentric - Endocentric
- Xenogenous (originating from outside) - Autogenous
- Xerothermic (adapted to dry heat) - Hygrothermal (adapted to wet conditions)
- Xenogenous - Autogenous
- Xenocrystic (relating to foreign crystals in geology) - Indigenous
- X-ray-visible - X-ray-opaque
- Xylocarpous (having a hard, woody fruit) - Non-woody
- Xenocentric - Egocentric
- Xenodochial (friendly to strangers) - Unwelcoming
- Xenogenic - Autogenic
- Xerothermic - Hydrophilic
- Xylophytic (wood-dwelling) - Non-wood-dwelling
- Xenotropic (preferring foreign environments) - Autochthonous (preferring native environments)
- Xylographic (related to wood engraving) - Non-graphic
- Xyloid (wood-like) - Non-wood-like
- Xenogeny (originating from foreign sources) - Autochthony (originating from native sources)
- Xanadu (pleasurable) - Dreary
- Xylophagous (wood-eating) - Non-xylophagous
- Xerothermic - Mesothermic
- Xenotime (a rare mineral) - Common
- Xylocarp (a type of fruit) - Non-fruit

- Zealous - Apathetic
- Zany - Serious
- Zestful - Unenthusiastic
- Zippy - Dull
- Zonal - Central
- Zonal (related to zones) - Non-zonal
- Zenithal - Nadir
- Zodiacal - Non-zodiacal
- Zany - Normal
- Zephyrous (like a gentle breeze) - Stormy
- Zonal - Non-zonal
- Zymotic (related to fermentation) - Non-fermentative
- Zebra-striped - Solid-colored
- Zealful - Indifferent
- Zygomatic (relating to the cheekbone) - Non-facial
- Zippy - Slow
- Zonal - Uniform
- Zesty - Mild
- Zapped (exhausted) - Energized
- Zoned - Unrestricted
- Zany - Conventional
- Zany - Staid
- Zany - Traditional
- Zen - Agitated
- Zany - Predictable
- Zinc-plated - Non-coated
- Zonal - Non-regional
- Zoological - Botanical
- Zodiacal - Non-astrological
- Zesty - Bland
- Zoned - Integrated
- Zealous - Disinterested
- Zoning - Open
- Zymotic - Stable
- Zigzag - Straight

# Table of Verbs (V1, V2, V3, V4, V5 forms)

| V1 (Base) | V2 (Past) | V3 (Past Participle) | V4 (Present Participle) | V5 (Third Person Singular) |
|---|---|---|---|---|
| accept | accepted | accepted | accepting | accepts |
| achieve | achieved | achieved | achieving | achieves |
| add | added | added | adding | adds |
| advise | advised | advised | advising | advises |
| agree | agreed | agreed | agreeing | agrees |
| allow | allowed | allowed | allowing | allows |
| ask | asked | asked | asking | asks |
| attack | attacked | attacked | attacking | attacks |
| avoid | avoided | avoided | avoiding | avoids |
| bake | baked | baked | baking | bakes |
| become | became | become | becoming | becomes |
| begin | began | begun | beginning | begins |
| believe | believed | believed | believing | believes |
| borrow | borrowed | borrowed | borrowing | borrows |
| bring | brought | brought | bringing | brings |
| build | built | built | building | builds |
| buy | bought | bought | buying | buys |

| V1 (Base) | V2 (Past) | V3 (Past Participle) | V4 (Present Participle) | V5 (Third Person Singular) |
|---|---|---|---|---|
| call | called | called | calling | calls |
| choose | chose | chosen | choosing | chooses |
| come | came | come | coming | comes |
| compare | compared | compared | comparing | compares |
| create | created | created | creating | creates |
| cry | cried | cried | crying | cries |
| cut | cut | cut | cutting | cuts |
| dance | danced | danced | dancing | dances |
| decide | decided | decided | deciding | decides |
| do | did | done | doing | does |
| draw | drew | drawn | drawing | draws |
| dream | dreamed/dreamt | dreamed/dreamt | dreaming | dreams |
| drive | drove | driven | driving | drives |
| eat | ate | eaten | eating | eats |
| embrace | embraced | embraced | embracing | embraces |
| enjoy | enjoyed | enjoyed | enjoying | enjoys |
| enter | entered | entered | entering | enters |
| erase | erased | erased | erasing | erases |
| examine | examined | examined | examining | examines |
| exist | existed | existed | existing | exists |
| expand | expanded | expanded | expanding | expands |

| V1 (Base) | V2 (Past) | V3 (Past Participle) | V4 (Present Participle) | V5 (Third Person Singular) |
| --- | --- | --- | --- | --- |
| Fall | fell | fallen | falling | falls |
| Feel | felt | felt | feeling | feels |
| Fight | fought | fought | fighting | fights |
| Find | found | found | finding | finds |
| Fly | flew | flown | flying | flies |
| Forget | forgot | forgotten | forgetting | forgets |
| Forgive | forgave | forgiven | forgiving | forgives |
| Freeze | froze | frozen | freezing | freezes |
| Get | got | gotten/got | getting | gets |
| Give | gave | given | giving | gives |
| Go | went | gone | going | goes |
| Grow | grew | grown | growing | grows |
| Hang | hung | hung | hanging | hangs |
| Have | had | had | having | has |
| Hear | heard | heard | hearing | hears |
| Help | helped | helped | helping | helps |
| Hide | hid | hidden | hiding | hides |
| Hit | hit | hit | hitting | hits |
| Hold | held | held | holding | holds |
| Hop | hopped | hopped | hopping | hops |
| Hurt | hurt | hurt | hurting | hurts |

| V1 (Base) | V2 (Past) | V3 (Past Participle) | V4 (Present Participle) | V5 (Third Person Singular) |
|---|---|---|---|---|
| Identify | Identified | Identified | Identifying | Identifies |
| Imagine | Imagined | Imagined | Imagining | Imagines |
| Improve | Improved | Improved | Improving | Improves |
| Include | Included | Included | Including | Includes |
| Inform | Informed | Informed | Informing | Informs |
| Insist | Insisted | Insisted | Insisting | Insists |
| Introduce | Introduced | Introduced | Introducing | Introduces |
| Invite | Invited | Invited | Inviting | Invites |
| Jump | Jumped | Jumped | Jumping | Jumps |
| Keep | Kept | Kept | Keeping | Keeps |
| Know | Knew | Known | Knowing | Knows |
| Laugh | Laughed | Laughed | Laughing | Laughs |
| Learn | Learned/Learnt | Learned/Learnt | Learning | Learns |
| Leave | Left | Left | Leaving | Leaves |
| Lend | Lent | Lent | Lending | Lends |
| Listen | Listened | Listened | Listening | Listens |
| Look | Looked | Looked | Looking | Looks |
| Love | Loved | Loved | Loving | Loves |
| Make | Made | Made | Making | Makes |
| Meet | Met | Met | Meeting | Meets |
| Move | Moved | Moved | Moving | Moves |

| V1 (Base) | V2 (Past) | V3 (Past Participle) | V4 (Present Participle) | V5 (Third Person Singular) |
|---|---|---|---|---|
| Need | Needed | Needed | Needing | Needs |
| Open | Opened | Opened | Opening | Opens |
| Organize | Organized | Organized | Organizing | Organizes |
| Play | Played | Played | Playing | Plays |
| Put | Put | Put | Putting | Puts |
| Quit | Quit | Quit | Quitting | Quits |
| Read | Read | Read | Reading | Reads |
| Ride | Rode | Ridden | Riding | Rides |
| Ring | Rang | Rung | Ringing | Rings |
| Rise | Rose | Risen | Rising | Rises |
| Run | Ran | Run | Running | Runs |
| Say | Said | Said | Saying | Says |
| See | Saw | Seen | Seeing | Sees |
| Sell | Sold | Sold | Selling | Sells |
| Send | Sent | Sent | Sending | Sends |
| Set | Set | Set | Setting | Sets |
| Sew | Sewed | Sewn | Sewing | Sews |
| Shake | Shook | Shaken | Shaking | Shakes |
| Shine | Shone | Shone | Shining | Shines |
| Shoot | Shot | Shot | Shooting | Shoots |
| Show | Showed | Shown | Showing | Shows |

| V1 (Base) | V2 (Past) | V3 (Past Participle) | V4 (Present Participle) | V5 (Third Person Singular) |
| --- | --- | --- | --- | --- |
| Shut | Shut | Shut | Shutting | Shuts |
| Sing | Sang | Sung | Singing | Sings |
| Sink | Sank | Sunk | Sinking | Sinks |
| Sit | Sat | Sat | Sitting | Sits |
| Sleep | Slept | Slept | Sleeping | Sleeps |
| Slide | Slid | Slid | Sliding | Slides |
| Speak | Spoke | Spoken | Speaking | Speaks |
| Spend | Spent | Spent | Spending | Spends |
| Spill | Spilled/Spilt | Spilled/Spilt | Spilling | Spills |
| Stand | Stood | Stood | Standing | Stands |
| Steal | Stole | Stolen | Stealing | Steals |
| Stick | Stuck | Stuck | Sticking | Sticks |
| Sting | Stung | Stung | Stinging | Stings |
| Stride | Strode | Stridden | Striding | Strides |
| Strike | Struck | Struck | Striking | Strikes |
| Swim | Swam | Swum | Swimming | Swims |
| Take | Took | Taken | Taking | Takes |
| Teach | Taught | Taught | Teaching | Teaches |
| Tear | Tore | Torn | Tearing | Tears |
| Tell | Told | Told | Telling | Tells |
| Think | Thought | Thought | Thinking | Thinks |

| V1 (Base) | V2 (Past) | V3 (Past Participle) | V4 (Present Participle) | V5 (Third Person Singular) |
|---|---|---|---|---|
| Throw | Threw | Thrown | Throwing | Throws |
| Understand | Understood | Understood | Understanding | Understands |
| Wake | Woke | Woken | Waking | Wakes |
| Wear | Wore | Worn | Wearing | Wears |
| Win | Won | Won | Winning | Wins |
| Write | Wrote | Written | Writing | Writes |

## "Examples of Verb Usage Across Tenses: Take"

**V1 (Base Form): Take**
- Simple Present: I take my dog for a walk every morning.

**V2 (Past Simple): Took**
- Past Simple: She took a day off yesterday to relax.

**V3 (Past Participle): Taken**
- Present Perfect: He has taken the train to work every day this week.

**V4 (Present Participle): Taking**
- Present Continuous: They are taking a trip to the mountains this weekend.

**V5 (Third Person Singular): Takes**
- Simple Present: She takes yoga classes every Friday.

# Conclusion

As you reflect on your progress, remember that learning a language is not merely about memorizing rules and structures; it is about embracing a new way of expressing yourself and understanding others. By immersing yourself in English through listening, speaking, reading and writing, , , you will continue to refine your skills and deepen your understanding.

The knowledge gained from this book serves as a springboard for your ongoing language journey. Whether you aspire to pursue higher education, advance in your career, or simply connect with people from diverse backgrounds, your proficiency in English will open doors to endless opportunities.

We hope that this book has empowered you to communicate confidently, expressively, and effectively in English. Remember, the journey of learning never truly ends—it evolves, adapts, and enriches your life in countless ways.

Keep learning, keep growing, and keep communicating. Your mastery of the English language is a testament to your dedication, persistence, and passion for learning. Now, go forth and let your words illuminate the world!
Wishing you success and fulfillment on your language learning journey,

Zeenam

**This book is available for purchase online on leading platforms.**

- **Amazon**: [My English Prof.-A comprehensive ESL Guide _ by ZEENAM IRSHAD].
- 
- **Flipkart**:[My English Prof.-A comprehensive ESL Guide _ by ZEENAM IRSHAD].
- 

Thank you for supporting this book. Your reviews and feedback on these platforms are greatly appreciated!

**If you have any feedback, questions, or suggestions, feel free to get in touch with me at:**

✉ **Email: [myeslprof@gmail.com]**

**Your input means a lot and helps me improve my future works. Thank you for your support!**

## Learn & Grow This Summer!

Looking to make your summer holidays both fun and productive? Join our Online English Classes designed to enhance your skills while enjoying the learning process.

⭐ Why Join Us?

- Interactive and engaging lessons.
- Perfect for students and professionals.
- Flexible schedules to fit your summer plans.